Writing
on the
Landscape

Other Books by Jennifer J. Wilhoit

Common Ground Between Crafts Collectives and Conservation (2008)

Weaving a Network (2009)

Writing
on the
Landscape

Essays and Practices to
Write, Roam, Renew

Jennifer J. Wilhoit, Ph.D.

LifeRich Publishing is a registered trademark of The Reader's Digest Association, Inc.

LifeRich Publishing books may be ordered through booksellers or by contacting:

LifeRich Publishing
1663 Liberty Drive
Bloomington, IN 47403
www.liferichpublishing.com
1 (888) 238-8637

ISBN: 978-1-4897-1410-7 (sc)
ISBN: 978-1-4897-1411-4 (hc)
ISBN: 978-1-4897-1409-1 (e)

Library of Congress Control Number: 2017955428

Print information available on the last page.

LifeRich Publishing rev. date: 09/25/2017

Dedication

For you, the writerly one

Contents

Acknowledgments

In order for this book to move from my inner landscape to the outer one, I needed the love and support of many dear ones. I so gratefully acknowledge:

My clients, who trust my guidance and courageously step into their deepest writing.

Bruce Rinker, astute scholar I deeply admire, who is a longtime champion of my writing and art.

Darcy Ottey, my writing partner, who shared, listened, and asked compelling questions as we wrote our way through our respective books.

Lisa McCall, my proofreader, whose passion for beauty imbues everything she does.

Stephen Jones, author and colleague, the first reader of this book and blurb writer extraordinaire.

My friends and family, who remind me of the preciousness of community—and Melissa Tran, who enthusiastically met my request for monthly check-ins during the book's homestretch; and Sheila Morehouse, who entrusted me with story-and-nature-guiding her loved one through an inordinately difficult life transition.

Mary Ann Daley, my mentor, whose compassionate wisdom sustains me through shadows and light.

Roger Moss, whose loving companionship is the very definition of the word "generous," and who is always ready to walk out into the landscape with me, Sage, and Ivory.

Chapter One

INVITATION

I invite you on this journey with me. I will guide you through writing and through experiences in nature. *Writing* is a process of getting what is inside of us into tangible form outside of us. *Nature* is both the actual landscape we see outdoors, as well as those rich natural tendencies in us that make us human. In this book, you will learn better how to explore what is within you and to express that in writing. You will also learn better how to explore the world of nature, which is always waiting to inspire, hold, and teach you. My hope is that you will come to experience for yourself how writing and the natural world are friendly to you. I have found that writing often, and spending time in nature regularly, add a fullness to my life—the sense that I am just a little bit more whole, more connected, and more peaceful than before I put pen to page or stepped outside.

What does it mean to find wholeness in writing or in the natural world? To whom or what do we turn for support when we feel we have nothing left to give to our particular writing project? Writing and nature are not mutually exclusive; in fact, they are partners in our quest for wholeness. Healing (which comes from the same root word as "whole") requires both inner and outer resources. What we contain and what contains us are in dynamic conversation. To be whole is to be reflective with perspective, to perceive the world with large eyes, to receive the world with a large heart. In short, when we can explore our inner and outer landscapes, recognizing how they are in fluid interplay one with the other, we are made more complete. It is such wholeness that this book seeks to inspire.

What does this wholeness have to do with writing? Read on. When we want to write something, we need balance of self and other.

We must first look within ourselves to see what is there (the wisdom, the beauty, even the pain) and to discover what we need. We reach into the depths of our stories and knowing, and do the inner research to arrive at the page with all that we can possibly know in a moment. We look outside of ourselves to remember that we are cared for, that something bigger than us exists to help meet our needs. We can also turn outside of ourselves—to the safety of nature—to find energy and insight when we can't find it easily within. We gather from our journeys into natural places the ability to see expansively. We also simply remember how our very breath is dependent upon the natural world; this roots us in collective knowing and creative inspiration that far surpass our individual knowledge.

We then turn to our writing—with the resources we've gathered from inside and outside of us—equipped with the tools we need to endure and complete our writing projects. That's when we are writing fully and honestly.

This book can help you do all of these. You will see many examples, through the essays here and by making a commitment to the writing-based and earth-based practices, of how our writing is made more complete when we arrive at the page with the fullness of ourselves.

This book is, first and foremost, for anybody seeking a way to balance their life in service to their writing, anyone who cares about wholeness. It is for the person who just wants to write, regardless of genre. This book is also for people who "have to" write (for school, business, profession) but who find writing totally arduous, frustrating, impossible to start, or intolerable to finish. The text here is for anybody who loves, or fears, the natural world and seeks a way to deepen relationship with it. The book offers itself to those who want to use writing as an exploration of the world, or themselves; it is also in service to those who already know how writing can save their lives but perhaps need additional motivation to sustain their writing practice. It is for anybody who loves sunlight on water or raindrops in the forest, anyone who sees how a journal entry can change the course of their day. And, this book is for anybody who wants a companion that has found solace and guidance in both her writing and the natural world. Dear reader, this book is from me to you.

Personal Experience

I spent decades having experiences that support, inform, and have inspired this book. At each of those points on my journey, though, all I knew is that I was having a powerful experience; I allowed myself, simply, *to be immersed* in them. It was not until somewhat recently that I followed the path of these markers, that I traced the trail from one experience to the next, that I actually had insight about how these experiences informed the work and passions I engage today. That is, experience came before knowledge for me. I had to live my way into my writing.

Writing saved my life. Engaging with the natural world toward greater wholeness and expression of my full self in the world saved my life. Writing and nature together have created the foundation for who I am: my well-being and health, my professional work for the world, my volunteerism in my community. I could not be who I am today without a fierce surrender to all that is natural—inside and outside of me. I would not be who I am today without a tender wrangling with words in the form of essays, papers, scholarly writing, books, blogs, poetry, and manuscripts of many other textures.

Recently I was reminiscing about how at each of the crucial writing stages in my life, I have turned to other sources and means of creative expression to support the writing challenges I was facing.

- When I was twelve years old—with a too-big assignment of a twenty-page story due for school—I found myself confused about how to end it. I decided to take a break. For the next several days, I continued to immerse myself in the out of doors; I biked, walked, played tennis. I played handbells at my church. I made more of the vivid drawings I had been doing since I was old enough to hold a crayon. And I already understood by that age how my dreams worked on me as I slept. So I also paid attention to my dreams; a few nights later, I dreamed the ending to my assigned story.

- The summer and fall before my thirtieth birthday, I went on a months-long bicycle trip to immerse myself in writing and nature. My bicycle was my "vehicle"; my tent was my "home"; nature was my "sanctuary"; and playing in sand and rock was my "art": all of it was inspiration for writing. I filled many journals with natural history facts, travelogue notes, daily insights, children's stories, and lots of sappy poetry.

- Working on my portfolio at the end of my bachelor's degree, I turned to a garden bed as my creative outlet while toiling over my writing.
- To help myself finish my master's degree, I bought a loom and took a weaving class. The creative processes I engaged as I wove textiles helped me finish writing my thesis.
- During the last aching throes of my doctoral work, I turned to watercolors and collage to sustain my writing. I enjoyed two international painting tours in the months leading up to the completion of my final dissertation draft.
- While writing this book, I have turned back to knitting—opting to take private instruction to push my skills to the next level. During quiet moments most days I also enjoy the spontaneity of working in my creative journal. I have recently—after a decades-long hiatus—rejoined a carillon choir. I also sustain my writing through daily hikes and walks, and creating nature altars on Earth holidays (like equinoxes and solstices).

It is no mistake that I have combined exploration of the natural world and creative pursuits as I finish up these huge writing projects in my life. They go hand in hand. I have learned how to pause, to let the I-don't-know-where-to-go-next-in-the-writing-project germinate. As I roamed the trails of the regional park the morning before writing this chapter, I loosely held in mind the next steps in the drafting of this book. As my eyes caught sight of birds, the glint of light on the oak leaves, the way the shadows created a mosaic of patterns on the ground, and felt the breeze cooling me off in the rising heat of the day—I was able to see, too, the shapes, colors, textures, light, and shadows in this manuscript. Walking out into the natural landscape affords me a vaster view of my inner landscape: that place from which my writing is born.

Not *the* Model, *a* Model

I present here one model for moving through writing and self. This book is not an all-inclusive tome, nor does it suggest that there is only a single route to writing from the wholeness of ourselves. This is "a" model, not "the" model. It is a set of practices that began with my personal writing, became well-honed as I moved through academic research writing, and has taken a clear shape in my professional writing. But the reason I write this book is not simply because the model, the practices, help *me*. I have seen over the years how these practices help my clients, the people who come to me for writing or life support. It has been my great privilege to guide people deeply within themselves so that they can write with clarity, so that they can move through and successfully finish a writing project that once stumped them. I have seen how writing has helped these clients find self-awareness. It is a dynamic process: writing leads us into ourselves, and it leads us back out again. Nature does so also.

Practices

What is a practice? Why do we do it? And, how does a writer engage practices that lead her deeper into her own journey and, thus, her story?

Here's an example of a land-based practice that led to a deepening of my personal story:

> I stooped down to put my hands gently upon the dried-up, late summer grass in the backyard of an adorable cottage that we rented. It was in a desert landscape, though ample watering could turn a small patch of dirt into a fairly lush lawn in winter months. I wondered how long I would be willing to use the earth's supply of water in that way, despite the homeowners' plea to keep the grass green. As I felt the prickles of the dry blades of grass on the tender skin of my palms, I was cognizant that I was engaging in a "practice": a simple act that is repetitive, intentional, meaningful. I felt good about the earth on which I lived, even though desert areas are not my habitat of choice. After several minutes of feeling the straw, the bone-dry dirt in which it was rooted, the texture of sand mixed in with the dirt, I knew what I had to do: to cease watering in spite of the landlord, in honor of the drought that plagued the area. The result of placing my hands

on the ground every day for over two years led me to an important turning point in my own story: deeper respect of the nonhuman world that is at the center of my values, profession, and spirituality, by reducing overconsumption of water in a painfully dry locale.

A practice is something we do, and do again, *repeating* with a rhythm that resounds over time. We practice to become better at something. My daily practice—now more than four years old (nearly fifteen hundred repetitions)—of placing my hands on the ground, enables me to more clearly remember, to feel, to improve my ability to connect with the earth. I am of the earth. As are you. But this placing of hands face down (or sometimes face up) on the earth outside—in every season, over and over and over again—grounds me on the inside, too. It leads me back to the soil of my inner landscape, reminding me that I am inextricably part of this vast earth (and that without her I would not be able to exist, to live, to be).

Placing my hands down on grass, dirt, mud, on beaches or rocks, on tree bark and roots, underneath the fallen leaves, on mosses and mushrooms and shrubs and pine needles, deep into icy pools of water or atop the newly fallen snow is a practice. I have the *intention* of improving my relationship to the planet—its landscapes and nonhuman living beings—each time my hands reach toward soil.

And this practice is deeply *meaningful* for me to the extent that I am compelled to change my behavior when my actions feel inconsistent with respecting Earth's resources and all who depend upon them. It moves, deepens, and roots me. It connects me with all that is alive, or dead and fallen, or desiccated, or verdant.

Why do I practice this? I do so to remember that I cannot live without the air, heat of the sun, and nourishment of plants that grow on this earth. I do so, also, to remember that my inner landscape needs the beauty, renewal, and cycles of the earth; they nourish my soul. I practice placing my hands in the rain puddle or tide pool so I remember each and every day that I can not live without water. I place my hands down so that I can surrender to all that is greater than me. I put my fingers deep into the tall, sweeping meadow grasses so that I can feel what is alive there, growing, moving, crawling—perhaps even clambering up my arm as I linger there, stooped. I crouch and then lie face down on the ground so that I can remember that this life is a gift and I am only here because nonhuman earthly things sustain me. Too, I crawl onto the earth outside my home or at the park or in the wilderness, using knees as conveyance, and I am reunited with the fact of my mortality: that my body will die. That is, I do so to savor this one precious moment that I can safely call "my life." This practice is my very lifeblood now: the flowing nourishment I need to make it through any moment, every crisis, each day, and to celebrate all that is this bounty we call "living."

How do I practice this groundedness? I do so by the actual act of going outside each and every day for the last four years, in each season, and in every type of weather, in different geographies in which I've lived, as well as in other countries, states, cities to which I have traveled in more than forty-eight months. I move my body outside of the shelter in which I am staying for that day and I bend over to sink my hands down into the vibrancy of nature. I stay there for a while, sometimes a few seconds or an hour. I am present during these moments: aware of what I am touching, how it feels on my fingertips, what the air is like, how chilled or warm I am, where I am, what I am touching and how it got there, what it offers in its sheer presence. Sometimes I cast my worries into the soil via the felt-connection I have as I touch dirt. Sometimes I say a short prayer of thanks or ask a question about my life. Other times I just do this practice with little feeling at all, as a commitment to the practice, because I have decided I will do so no matter where I am and how "busy" my life feels.

Of course, I have practices that I do for my writing, too.

Daily journaling is the sustenance for my writing. It is usually not the substance for what I write, but it frees me of the everyday mundane worries, tasks, or expectations that can constrain the content of my professional work. Writing in my journal in the dark early morning purges the beasts of nighttime dreams, loosens the memories of childhood, charts the day's course, nurtures hopes for the future, helps me contemplate the present. Journaling for me is the very essence of being in the moment: my pen is in my right hand moving across the page as if my very life depended on it. Which it does. Certainly my formal writing depends on this emancipation of my brain, the release of constriction of my heart; for when these are tight, there is no walking freely into the writing that is my gift to the world. The practice of journaling is my gift to myself.

Practices, whether nature- or writing-based, have a larger-than-life intention. They unfold the wrinkles in our thinking, the crimps in our soul, the catch in our throat, and they give us permission to pronounce ourselves ready for the real work of the day.

This book offers both the earth-based and writing-based practices with the aim of providing to you the "what" of your writing: content, process. But these are empty without a life that supports writing; the practices in this book also aim to guide you toward greater depth, response to, and peaceful engagement with your actual, daily life.

All of the practices in this book should be done alone.

By yourself.

In a quiet place.

With no electronics visible or audible.

Relationship with self requires spending time with oneself. We must take time for solitude, self-reflection, quiet. Introverts need solitude in order to recharge; we all need time alone in order to know ourselves better. This is increasingly difficult to achieve with electronics that can alert us to every "Like," "Retweet," or "Skills Endorsement." It is impossible to avoid noticing the arrival of an email or text message; even with the phone muted, there is the potential for the telltale "vibration" sound or lit up screen catching our attention. Turning off the phone, stowing it in a room far away, or locking it inside the car while we are on a trail are great options for keeping others out of our private time. Nobody is welcome to join us when we are doing the practices in this book. Anytime we answer—or even read—a message on one of our devices while we are engaged in writing or time in nature, we have let somebody in to our private space. I can hear some readers balking at these words. Unplugging is so unpopular! And ... it is absolutely necessary for nurturing and deepening our relationship with ourselves and with the fullness of our human nature.

Think about it this way: If you wanted to get to know a romantic interest better, to have a private conversation with him or her, would you really invite your parents along or your entire circle of friends? Likely not. This is exactly what I'm referring to throughout this book when I suggest spending time with yourself: it is an intimate affair. To really know ourselves as part of the natural world, to get to the real heart of our writing, we must dig deeper—exploring the cavernous terrain of self: inner and outer. This can only happen when we take time to get to know who we really are from moment to moment, year to year, experience by experience.

Essay: I'd Rather Write

Generally, I need to begin my writing first thing in the morning. That is how it used to be, anyway. Writing patterns shift as life moves and changes. What is most crucial for me now is to be in the right mindset. This actually means being in the right "heartset": having a clear, open pathway to my heart so that I can write in an impassioned way about my passions. It might also mean writing about things with which I am not so enthralled—as long as I find that one small hunk of a thing that is interesting, and conjure it into a passion. Trickery is fine in writing: whatever we can do to get ourselves to the page is good.

Yesterday I was distracted by "life" and did not write; the whole day I was on the road, driving and searching, figuring and discussing. Not one scrap of it had anything to do with this book. I spent today editing somebody else's work to meet their deadline. Now it is late in the day and I feel edgy, antsy. It is nearly quitting time for today and I'm just sitting down here to write. Why? Because I needed to clear the decks of other responsibilities and deadlines. I cannot write freely—in a landscape of wide roamingness—if I have other pressing deadlines. It just won't work.

But right now the ease of writing is mine. All mine. All of a sudden I feel excited, hungry to write all that is ready to soak the page with its wet newness. Like the dawn's dew as I run my fingers across leaves, the dog's fur after she's pranced through rain, or the silky tenderness of a rose petal, I am tantalized by the tactile sensation of writing. I can write as little or as long as I like. I can compose anything I want to. I can tell the reader all those things I have longed to write since I was the small girl of twelve, disbelieving that I could ever write something longer than the "thank you" notes my mom made me write to relatives upon receiving holiday gifts.

I rather write now than anything else in the whole world. It is true.

I feel I have earned the right to write, an inheritance that began in my cells long before consciousness was mine. I bear within myself a legacy passed down from several relatives on my mother's side; these family members yearned to write but never did. Now, all I want to do is while away the days typing as much and as fast as I can. I do not have any time to lose, and have more to write than I could possibly manage in a few lifetimes. I started writing late—late today, and late in my life. At least, the latter is true if only publications matter; journaling has been my companion for more than forty years. My ancestors did not take their rightful place in the world of writing, nor did they publish; I do not want to waste my genetic chance.

As much as I love this earth, this land so verdant or dry, supple or waning, vast and diverse and supportive of all biological life—as much as all that passion, I am imbued with an earthy urge to write. I would rather write than work on anything else. Anything.

There are countless journeys to be experienced on the land. Rivers course and rafts rush down their white rapid riffles. Mountains with achingly sweet curves and secret hiding spots tantalize hikers and view-seekers. Desert rocks or vast stretches of Saharan solitude beckon to some who find prayer and plentitude in the ever-shifting sands of white-hot survival. One human might choose to bask or bawl in the cloistered, dark dampness of a rainforest, or howl with the coyotes on a new moon in June. Winterscapes call to the ice and snow enthusiasts, fast or slow going on skis, sleds, boards, shoes ... or to those who loaf by fires who want only the romantic snowflake view. Meadows filled with wildflowers, wetlands stirred by the waters feeding their mucky hollows, tree-lined paths or ocean waves, there is movement and life and some of those are *Homo sapiens* doing what we do all over this broad planet of experience.

We write ourselves all over this earth, in ways destructive and healing, in the spirit of arrogant "dominion over" or in respectful supplication; as environmental activists, healers, oil diggers, tree huggers and cutters, policymakers, developers, low-impact-off-the-grid-bare-minimum-low-consumer-simple-living folks, scientists, artists, and some—perhaps many—who really do not care for much at all that resides outside their electronic immersion. We humans write ourselves all over the place whether we think about it, intend to, or not. Just breathing the air as living humans, there is a footprint, a cost, a beauty, and a little death in the life of each being.

Writing our way through life, or riding our way through, we cannot deny the fact—even though most of us do—that we are imbedded in one another and this earth. And I would rather write. I would rather write than edit. I would rather write than sing. I would rather write than listen to music, or run errands, or pay bills, or clean the bathroom. I would rather write on the land leaning against a tree with butterflies and soft leafy breezes as my sole distractions. Writing and the earth go together. Hand in hand. Or, they can. It is this that I want to encourage through this book: to find our own way back through the denial, or distraction, through the deadlines and obligations, right back to the core of hearty truth. The best way I know how to do this is through vital, alive writing that breathes as I do, that hurts and giggles and whispers too loudly or yells too softly. We each have a role to play on this planet. It is not a role like an actor in a play. It is a part in the whole scheme. It is a vital breath that we offer through our work, our holy calling to be whomever we can be when we serve from our fullest and most burning hot loves. We each offer to others our breath, our service, our work.

And I mean you, too.

It does not matter whether you know "how" to write, it only matters that we practice writing. I recall that first writing I did as a preschooler; my crayons and colored pens made wavy up and down strokes—all connected one hump to the next—and I called it "writing." It was my child's way of copying the beautiful handwriting I saw everyday: that of my mom's right-tilted slant and squared off edges of her left-handed script. Whether or not the writing task that faces you is personal or formal, required or frivolous, it is not in vain, or worthless, or empty. Said another way: there is pure value in every word you write.

Each word is a breath. It is the mouth opening onto the page, to say whatever is begging to be heard by the world around the writer. Every sentence is an idea the earth and her inhabitants have been waiting to receive since the moment you took your first inhalation. Writing and the earth are the birthrights of each human being. My dog is one of the most precious beings in my world. For all her intelligence, spunk, lovingkindness, and adorability, she cannot write. Just the fact of our humanity—this hand and this brain converging in the body of landscape we call "a human"—should be enough to stir each person right out of his stupor, amnesia, overcomplicated "life" and back into the amazing gift we were given: the ability to write. It is a miracle really.

Writing can be a refuge, a safety, the clear still waters that spill forth to give new life. It can be a passion and lifesaver. It can teach us and teach others. Writing takes infinite forms and is as diverse as the biological bliss of life on this planet. Writing is as bright as the stars, as deep as the ocean, as hot as the sun, as solid as rocks, as explosive as volcanoes, as shakeable as earthquakes, as beautiful or dingy or tattered or fresh as a writer needs it to be. Yes, writing is a choice. The content is a choice. The form is a choice. The willingness to do it or not is a choice. So, as much as we have this grand capability that no other living beings can accomplish in quite the same way, too, we have to make a decision about whether or not to tap our capacity to write.

Each of us has a unique potential, a tiny twinkling of something burning way down in our guts. It might emerge as bile or praiseful poetry, as a burp or searing prose. The outcome won't matter at first. Simply, one must begin by picking up a pen or putting fingers on the keyboard, and just seeing what happens. We are not all inspired. We are not all poets. We are not all book writers or essayists, columnists or scholars or sermon-makers, or perfectly tidy in how we write.

What matters beyond anything is that we give writing a shot. Over and over. One really good effort and then another. For the reader who has started on this journey with me, please remember that there is one gold ring for every attempt you make at writing. It is true. One gold ring per practice. It does not have to be shiny, perfectly circular, yellow or white or pink or green, new or untried, elaborate or tight or just right or loose. The déjà vu I have as I write those words recall to mind another essay from many years ago in which I probably beseeched the reader to consider the very same idea I write here now seven years and eons of learning later: just write.

I could weep with all the years of waste during which I did not write, yet felt so utterly compelled and called to it. Even if the person who needs (but doesn't want) to write can sit down and compose one single sentence that is durable—that has as its backbone any measure of real honesty—she will steady herself in her own story. She will pull her way along to the next sentence, and the next.

There are so many excuses for not writing. But I would rather write than anything else because it is a way to move across the landscape of self; yes, for me it is an indulgent and selfish act to write. I see no one and I hear nothing when I am at the computer or have a journal in my lap. Even sometimes when I am out in the world just prior to or following a writing session, I see nothing and hear nobody. But this is okay because I am listening to what is going on inside me during those writing sessions. Like each small stitch in knitting adds up to a row and then becomes five rows, suddenly I've got some swatch of a thing that could be warm and cozy—or just a bit too coarse and itchy; but I have *some*thing, at least. And, like knitting, I feel earthy and wholesome when I write.

Often, I don't quite know what is going to scare me onto the page or off it again. I do not know what the outcome will be. It. Doesn't. Matter.

Writing will never happen by itself. That is a guarantee. This was the profound and most devastating blessing of my graduate work: that decisive moment when I knew I could not finish my degree unless I sat down every day and put some words, however clumsy or irrelevant, onto the page. Anything would do, as a start. Something would shift. The force of impact hit me, knocked me around: no matter how arduous and inconceivable, I was absolutely the only person in the whole world who could earn myself the three letters after my name that I thought would save my life. The truth is, those credentialing letters did not save my life. It was the *writing* I did —and continue to do—that saves my life again and again, and over again one more time.

I can absolutely promise you that if you want to write, or need to badly enough, there will be a way through. May these practices be a start for you, a new life, a lifesaving gesture that gives you hope.

Structure of the Book

The first two chapters introduce the ideas that are fundamental to this book: that one way of navigating our writing projects is by focusing on the processes that can sustain us over time. Specifically, we do so by calling on a source greater than ourselves to sustain, motivate, inspire, and teach us: that of body earth. In short, writing from a lifestyle grounded in nature is a bona fide means for such.

The next four chapters offer inspiration and guidance for how to engage twelve writing and nature practices that are considered foundational for grounded writing; six of these involve free-writes, journaling, and tasks to help structure the writing content and process, while the other six ask the aspiring writer to engage an activity or routine out in the natural world. These four chapters each pair a way of perceiving and receiving the world with one of four earth elements. Chapter 3 is focused on the body of human and the element of earth, while the fourth chapter looks at the role of emotion and the element of water. The fifth chapter moves into an exploration of mind paired with air. And Chapter 6 brings in spirit and the element of fire. So, together, we will engage our: physical bodies on the body of earth, emotional states through the lens of water, knowledge-building as the breath of our writing content, and the fiery passion of inspiration. These four parts of ourselves—body, emotion, mind, spirit—are integral and in service to our writing. The four elements—earth, water, air, fire—are integral to nature and support us as part of that web. These designations are not mutually exclusive or all-inclusive; they are *one* way of working with ourselves and nature toward a sustainable writing practice and life.

The last chapter revisits what wholeness means in regard to writing and life, sums up the ideas offered in this book, and issues a call for commitment to oneself and one's writing.

The directions for each practice are meant to inform and support the writer. There are essays that support the ideas inherent in the practices, as well as step-by-step directions for engaging each practice. In fact, I offer the reader a "medium" practice but also offer tips for easier ("gentler") or more challenging ("deeper") levels of each practice. If the standard practice feels too daunting, begin with the "gentler" practice. If the standard practice is not that different from how you already engage writing or the natural world, then choose the deeper practice. There's no right or wrong way to begin; the point is simply to engage in the first place.

For it is through actively writing that we learn how to write, and it is through using various forms of writing that we learn better about our writing process. This is true in learning to experience the riches of nature as well: through spending time in nature we become more comfortable there which increases our willingness to explore landscapes more deeply.

While I do not ask the reader to take long wandering hikes for hours at a time or to do a wilderness trek or fast, I do offer options for developing intimacy with the natural world ... and thus, with yourself. This can be done in the course of our daily activities and responsibilities, and without going too far away. Writing experience and nature experience move us deeper into our lives. This book offers ways to do so.

Getting Started

Feel free, of course, to engage this book in whatever manner suits you. While I wrote this with the intention that the reader start at the beginning and read chronologically to the end, some readers will jump in at the point where the practices begin in each chapter. For the reader who is not quite ready to engage the practices, see if you can open your heart to the essays in this book. Find what you have in common with the experiences you read about on the page. Decide if you have enough at stake, or enough passion, to begin. Find the courage you need by immersing yourself in the natural history of the inner landscape as it is written about in the non-practices portions of this book. What I ask is that you choose what you need right now. Because writing is like that; it is a slippery thing that begs for our attention in one moment and pushes us away with its hard critiques the next. This book is here with you now; whatever you forego reading today will wait for you, will wait until you are ready to open.

For the reader who is willing to take on the practices in this book, I have some recommendations for getting started. What I mean by "getting started" is moving ahead with your writing process. I intend for the practices I offer in this book to be engaged repeatedly, over time, to become part of what someone does in order to sustain a writing practice over time. This book is about writing process as well as completion of a manuscript (or a series of writing projects/assignments).

Please remember: there is no substitute for writing. I went through a period of time during which I read many books about writing. Some had writing prompts (this book is very spare on writing prompts). Others focused on a particular genre (the practices here are useful regardless of the genre—scholarly, creative, business writing, personal). Still others contained advice about grammar, structure, rules. Or they focused on big themes like writing for social change, writing through grief, writing toward peace. But reading about writing is not writing. No matter how many great books I read, my writing never really shifted—and certainly my writing process could never develop into practices that could sustain me, and my writing projects—until I *actually put pen to page*. I mean this very literally:

I had to pick up a pen (not a pencil, which has an eraser, and fades to ghostlike script over time).

I had to have a sheaf of paper ready (mostly I choose sketchbooks because they are unlined and I prefer bound paper to loose leaf).

And, **I actually had to write across the page often** and with as much courage as I could muster.

We cannot begin, develop, or finish a writing project without writing. We cannot figure out how to make a life that includes writing (even if it is a temporary writing life—that of a student required to write papers each term, or a grandmother writing a memoir for her family) if we do not actually write something. Reading is not writing. Organizing is not writing. Learning is not writing. Taking a break is not writing. Speaking into a transcription device is not writing. All of these are *in service to* a written outcome. Some of these I even encourage in this book. But there is no substitute for putting words on a page via the movement of our hands.

With all this in mind, I encourage you to do three things before proceeding any further:

1.   Create a writing space in your home.

The writing area does not have to be fancy. It should be a place that is quiet and separated from the main hub of activity in your home. Ideally, it has a door that shuts and a surface upon which to write (desk, folding table). It is where you will spend most (if not all) of your writing time.

2.   Set a time to write.

Some people prefer to choose a particular time of day that is dedicated to writing. Others prefer to decide upon an amount of time each day that they will write. If you're not sure, try both; for example: I will write every Monday, Wednesday, and Friday from 8:00 to 9:00 AM.

3.   Commit to tidying up the writing space after every writing session.

Clients continually tell me that a barrier to sitting down to write is entering a writing space that contains yesterday's mess. At the end of each writing session, straighten the papers into a pile. Close the books over a bookmark and stack them. Remove any dishes and put away pens.

Allow me now to guide you through the writing process and through natural landscapes so that your courageous life can be shared on the page as a gift for the world.

Chapter Two

WRITING AND ECOLOGY

Essay: Twenty-Six Words

It all starts with about twenty-six words. Maybe they are sentences that the writer later deletes, once the flow and heart of the writing project begin to emerge. But those first words on the page string together into a line and a half of text that leads to more than half a page of text. This in turn becomes half a chapter and half a book, until finally the entire thing is fleshed out. But it is undeniably true: the essay or chapter or book or bio or résumé or thesis or blog entry or research paper will never come to fruition, will never literally (bear) *fruit*, until those first words hit the page. And perhaps the page isn't the first place they land.

Swirling inside the heart, something flutters—a twinkle of a feeling that a seed buried deep within just might have cracked its hull to reveal the surreal lime green potential of something. It can happen in the head too: a small tremor or Richter scale quake that shakes something loose, an edge of an idea. Then, as dreaming and working, walking and waiting, become the guiding events of each day, that tiny little leaf begins to stretch itself out and the surprising sharpness of the idea widens and reveals itself. It becomes part of one's being as the plant or fault line grow up, widen, within. When it ripens into the fullness of maturity it begins to call out for attention, craves a voice: this nudging for expression is the substance of the first twenty-six words.

The very first draft of the opening chapter of this book began with twenty-six words: "Introduction: Do you have to write something but feel stuck? Are you passionate about writing but never seem to get any words down on the page?" The heart-seed and mind-tremor began a good long gestational while before those words ever became manifest, black on white, on a page. More writing, rewriting, critiques, and layers of editing later those first twenty-six words may become parsed, replaced and overwritten (overridden) by a string of letters and words better suited to the overall gist of the book and the specific task of the chapter. Nevertheless, those important first words became the gateway, the path, the steppingstones to continue. Without twenty-six initial words, even in the interrogative form (questions to oneself or the reader), the fuller manuscript cannot take shape.

Twenty-six words: a website homepage, long text message, short email, handwritten thank you card, grocery list, recipe, vacation postcard, job description on a CV, Craigslist advertisement. These are ordinary, daily recordings—some typed, and some handwritten in ink so blue the writer wanders outside to gaze upon the remembered sky. Taking this a step further, twenty-six words is one quarter of a scholarly abstract; ten percent of a typewritten page; or, multiplied by forty-six, a New York Times newspaper article. Write this many words one hundred times and suddenly the author has scripted one third of a short story or two entire essays. From there it is only fifteen more chunks to a novel, or just seven to a novella.

That novella-seed might have started in a bubble bath two years ago. The op-ed piece might have sprung from two serrated words ("No *way!*") at the last town hall meeting. The dissertation was necessarily built block by arduous block from cycles of research and analysis, no mere child's tower to be sure. And the memoir came from heartache and surrender, or victory and celebration, or perhaps a dose of both in the leading lines of the manuscript.

*   *   *

The issue lies herein: while twenty-six words herald the onset of something powerful, mighty, and real, they scarcely leave the confines of the author-to-be's mind or heart all by themselves, without any effort on their behalf by a writerly person. There is a chasm. It is wide, with steep granite rock walls slippery with the moist, sometimes icy, build-up. And it is oh so deep, a thing of wonder, awe, and glory once it is overcome; but it is a thing of fierce tenacity before it is conquered. Yes, a conquest! This pit lies between the first heart- or head-stirrings and the actual carving out on a page. Like the ancients' communications on rock, mumbo jumbo hieroglyphics, beautiful, but which only bear meaning when the expert interprets them for the waiting listeners. It is the writer's courageous task to plumb the depths of this earth-vault so as to emerge with the precious gift of articulation. Between the infant whispers of an idea and the twenty-six miraculous first-words lies this traversable but highly risky cavern.

I have witnessed all sorts of chasms in others. Some stretch for miles, as the want-to-be author moves from geography to landscape, uprooting home and possessions and family in search of something he cannot find until he waters the page with his beginning: "I tell this story now because ... " Another person I know accumulates life experiences in grand and obscure places: racking up knowledge, invaluable explorations, a travel-savvy unmatched. But always she ends up at home, empty and despairing because there is no outlet to share the adventure; she is rooted no place because she is not rooted within herself. The rift between writing idea and expression can take the shape of decades, and this might be the riskiest one of all; as a longtime hospice volunteer I have heard many individuals give voice to the dream to write, but by the time I was honored to join their journey they were a long way beyond being able to do so. An equally trepidatious type of chasm is the one which reaches into the molten core of the earth and emerges with a fistful of fire. The blessing in the erupting volcano is that it is often powerful enough to send the writer right to the table with ash on her hands and a smoky taste in her mouth.

No matter the grit between our toes, the sand in our trouser cuffs, the stale breath on our tongues, as long as we make it to the writing page— putting down two-dozen and two words—we have earned the moniker, "hero."

I have personally experienced numerous and variable caverns in my own writing. Once, being so sure I would be successful, I announced to loved ones that I would attend the fated meeting on such and such date and from then-forward be called "candidate." How bitter and sticky was the citrus that lingered when I arrived at the meeting room of somber faces, an immediate sign that a victory was not yet mine. The only reprisal was to stand tall and firm, vowing to earn the coveted title no matter what hardship I endured. I thought I knew what I had to write, but the blazing hot distance between my expectation and the committee's took (literally) several months of test and error, scrutiny, drafts, edits and rewrites. My "twenty-six words" toward the end of that trial came in the form of one, gleaming, unexpectedly simple, meticulously crafted paragraph, one third of a page. (Incidentally, the other one hundred and seventy nine paragraph-sized wads of text that followed to complete the document were ones that I scrupulously—even painfully—cobbled together out of mimicry: *If this is the model that works to sate the approvers, then I will not err one centimeter from its form.*)

Prior to that bloody-knuckled experience, I had received the types of praise and evaluations of my work that anybody would be proud to claim. I didn't receive such kudos *every* time I wrote something, but certainly during particular periods of my life. High school papers and my master's degree essays, articles, thesis, and research were two such notable "wet periods" in my writing: times when the grading standards were high but during which I thrived and readily succeeded.

However, sometimes the line between idea and written word is etched in blood, fixed as if by divine order. During my first summer away at college, working a nose-pickingly, thumb-twiddlingly, boring administrative job in a back corner of the university library—escaping every weekend to sleep in the back seat of my Volkswagen bug by night and hike the sumptuous peaks of the Rockies by day—I thought I would write a book. About my family. "Our family story." I believe I managed to get about fourteen words onto the page, in the form of bullet point notes. Barrier after barrier arose within me, quickly whittling the list of topics down to about three. But none of those were my story to tell; they were about other family members' private lives. Fate intervened that time; I figured out that I was not ready, shrouded as I was in all my youthful naiveté, to take on the lives of six other people from whom I had not yet separated enough to have even a breath of hindsight, much less any type of story.

This also happened a few years later when I embarked on a novel writing course at the prestigious local university in the new city I had moved to; I just could not make up a story. For the life of me. I am, probably by some irrevocable trust between a Creator of the Universe and my very genes, not a fiction writer. I have known that now for a long time. But it took the sort of chasm that just closes up and disappears from the landscape altogether to teach me about my own writing direction.

Take comfort, dear aspiring writer. Though I am a daily writer now with a growing list of publications to my name, I have many more of these chasm-stories. If I can find my way to the page, so can you.

*   *   *

Each word of the first twenty-six requires a journey, one that is necessarily preceded by preparation (nurturing the spark of a written work) and followed by a commitment to travel the distance it takes to completion. What is the point of the nerve-grinding climb out of, the growing of wings to fly over, the boring into the mantle of the earth to tunnel through, the surrender of all things sane and rational, if the abiding pledge to ourselves and to the world stops across the other side of the abyss in the safety zone? The journey—however wide, deep, steep, or inclement the terrain—is only the arrival at the page. Real courage, true heroine-ism, the utter and undeniable pounding of the hammer on nail comes in the giving, the gifting, of our words to an audience. This means writing it down, fleshing it out. Whatever is required of a person to make it from inspiration to perspiration, so that the page falls like a promise into our laps, is just the beginning. There must be a compulsion: a grade or degree or certification or license that stands on the other side of the finished page, a major life change, the fear of not writing it at all becoming bigger than figuring out how to do so.

*   *   *

Now at the gateway, the writerly one pauses. Rests. She waits until she has caught her breath—marveling at the miracle of having arrived to the page, having faced and overcome the hurdles to actually get however-many-words-it-took from head and heart to black and white symbols on screen or paper. Reflection on the journey so far, a sketching out of the high and low points, childlike wonder and mature contemplation about how to proceed. All of this she does as her breath moves from gasps and pants to a slow, steady in ... and out again. The one who wants to write has just made a breathtaking journey, crawling through whatever it took in the biggest effort ever to craft an opening, to slice into the page. Just like the words that have emerged, just like the words that will proceed forward: the writer breathes them in, writes them out. Exhalation. Inspiration, respiration, aspiration. It would be foolhardy to stop now, to refuse the gifts of the journey that will become the gift of words to the world.

So the writer looks in front, ahead, off into the far distance. It is impossible to focus on the actual landing place, to know quite how the gift the traveler received will transform into the offering for the waiting reader. But in the foreground are a few recognizable landmarks, a way forward perhaps. Equipped with those initial lines of text, the once-seed-now-a-tiny-sapling, the writer inches forward. Sometimes a small skip or hop. But mostly just a precise—or haphazard—movement from one stone or marker or bush to the next. Hours or days might pass between each of these tiny but necessary accomplishments. Each is in service to the next. Each is crucial. Each will save the life of the writer, and probably the waiting world too. Every word, phrase, sentence, paragraph that the writer is compelled to inscribe *is* that sometimes-halting, sometimes-catapulting motion toward an end product. Whether the writing adventure is a hard-won paragraph for an assignment, the achievement of a lifetime graduate thesis, chapter one of the second novel, the restorying of professional life into the synopsis called a curriculum vitae, the long-awaited saga of a memoir, or an entirely *other* kind of written thing altogether, it is done in pieces. Stages, bits, hunks.

And the adhesive that glues it all together into a cohesive whole is the willingness of the writer to show up, present, aware, with as many layers of one's self intact as possible. That will does not resemble willfulness or selfishness or ego; neither does it wallow in self-interest. It might require stubbornness, fortitude, and strength. It necessarily mandates that the one who will write stir deep in her guts to scrape out the last drops of courage each time she faces The Blank Page. For the act of writing our passions, our compulsions, our callings is not solely for ourselves. Most of us do not possess a large enough, limitless enough, supply of stamina to write just for ourselves. At least not the type of writing that is a bridge between the depths of our own core and the soul of the reader. Putting into words on the glaringly stark white page for a readership our deeply honest work is really the willingness to share who we are. Unabashedly.

What sustains the willingness and the renewal of courage to pick up where we last left off with the writing is the faith that we will reach the obscure but sure, far-off horizon: that one we really cannot yet catch a glimpse of, but which we know must exist just on the other side of the river, down the valley, around that mountain over there and back behind the grove of trees nestled on the opposite slope. It is the faith that we were given this need to write (or assignment, task, storyline) for some reason. Maybe it is divine purpose. Or maybe it is simply the agonizing process of advancing toward an academic degree, earning the new job, winning over one's friends with the wow-of-a-fifty-thousand-word novel. Or maybe we intuitively know that our loved ones desperately need the wisdom and sapphire of that primal Story we have kept locked away inside the protective shield of our hearts, the one that might break our heart to tell again, but which will heal and hold and carry forward the precious reader. It is worth it if it heals.

During that time on the land, in areas that might not really feel familiar, somebody who writes must shed a few of the comforts, knowns, and givens. The blazing hot sun will drive the writer to rest in the blotchy shade of a lonely pine tree. The pathway she thought she should take might be filled with thorny brambles causing her to back up, start anew on a different course. Daily meals and routines, even a shower, might be obscure and decadent luxuries of the past or rewards of the future; writing sometimes asks us to snack at our desk through the lunch hour or forego that social opportunity just this once in order to stay in the wilderness of writing through another chapter's completion. Letting go the comforts of now so that words can arrange and rearrange in a document is okay. It is needed even. Knead, shape, roll back into a ball, and start again. Everything we think we need to do will absolutely prevent us from writing, especially the writing that can make-whole. There are things we will give up (including our thoughts about who we are as a writer and what our writing is or "should be"). There are things we will alter. There are also barriers that will loom large: a gravelly mountain slope down which we treacherously slide struggling for a foothold on the writing project, for example. Despite all this seeming-hardship, the writer perseveres. The goal is too enticing, or too much work has been put in to turn back now; either reason works. Somehow, we still have the faith even after a crummy, slow day at the keyboard.

What is known is there. It is inside of us. So it doesn't matter what has to be loosed or lassoed to keep us writing. We just know we must; sometimes that is all we feel we know.

The faith, hope, or covenant of writing is kept alive by the very pain that gives it birth. Without the once-in-a-while agony of deep writing, nothing real or truth-bearing, provocative or compelling, life-saving or culture-changing would ever, *ever* come into existence. But the pain only comes sometimes, and in doses. Unlike bearing young, a writer can actually shift the patterns of the discomfort, deplete some of the power, take some of the intensity out of the feelings that he finds intolerable as writing proceeds.

It is a long journey from the depths to the surface, but it is certainly not an insurmountable one if you carry with you faith and a few practices. The landscape is filled with songful praise for the writer. And I literally mean the landscape of this earth on which we live.

Essay: Connecting with the Land

I am sitting outside with the computer on my lap. A blue jay has just swept into the yard and eyes me from a perch atop the fencepost. I notice that his tail feathers and bright flash of wing bars are a deeper hue than the impossibly dark, powder blue of the hot sky. The day is not clear; splotches of white harmless clouds float gently above. Toward the south, the icing clouds are thick and spread out: a heavenly picnic blanket. Cicadas, or crickets—I'm not sure which—join with the songs, calls, and frivolous musings of the menagerie of bird life. That jay has come back and seems to taunt me by hiding in the top of a nearby tree calling for his life, with a voice too-loud to be emotionless. I am reminded of the dragonfly—that very tiny one I saw soaring five feet above the grassy field where my dog rolled, ran, frolicked, and chased.

In all of this I see myself: the desire to fly, to find the color and shape of my belonging. I see how I change form as I become impacted by the winds of my day. I spread out a cloth that is the lounging place in the tall grass; I find my voice by sometimes speaking louder than I intended. Sometimes my truth is my refuge as I write; even though, too, it can be the very thing that sends me running for refuge in the superficial. The truth of who we are is not always something we want to feel. And yet, we must if we are going to write.

Because we *are* nature. Natural. Of the earth.

I might happen to find insight or inspiration for writing in the very dirt of this yard, or in my region; I might find deep connection in travels to lands far off. After all, this entire planet on which I have sojourned—sinking my fingers into the silt, sand, or thick cold mud of places familiar *and* foreign—is our one home. I write from the very core of who I am. That is what the natural world does for me and for my writing no matter where I am. The more I connect with what *is*, the more I write from my deep-seeded soul. And the way that I can get to what *is* happens to be through connection with trees, grass, weeds, flowers I know or don't, the stagnant river alongside which the homeless are taking shelter, the memory of ocean waves from lifetimes of knowing, from the shell up to my ear, from images and imaginings of my own life and the tales others tell. Because—while there is constant flux, change, shift, movement, fluidity to the natural world, as well as in my own humanity—I find also the abiding constancy of it. In just the way that I wake up to the same orange, lemon and grapefruit trees standing in my backyard each morning, I awaken to my own natural abundance and continuity. It is not that I feel immortal as much as I feel deeply connected to all that is here now, will fade away, and that has been long before my short decades on earth came into consciousness.

In preparing to craft this essay, I wanted to write solely from that indelibly constant fact that is my nature, even in the face of the truth that I am just one, small, fleeting life. So I went outside into nature. Though a temporary resident of Earth, I can tap in to the constancy of all life through the everlasting presence of the natural world. Humans are connected by a web to all that lives, breathes, sighs, and cries. When I become weighed down by the worries of the day—small life details, all of the non-enduring events of my little life—I am behaving as if I am separate from that web of life.

I have thought about all the great, noteworthy, commendable, award winning, famous, meticulous writers I know. I wondered if they would agree with me that we must be connected to the natural world in order to write more honestly. The truth of our lives that shows up in our writing comes from being conscious of our interconnection with the complex and multilayered natural world. It does not matter whether or not we "feel," "sense," or "believe" it. We have, in this culture at least, been fed the lie until we are engorged by our own egos: that we are separate from and—worse yet—better than, superior to, in charge of, and more powerful than that which we have severed from and look outside ourselves at, what we have come to call "nature."

But if you are stuck, have reached an impasse in your writing, and are ready to step into the *process* of writing—whether out of intrinsic calling or external demand—you really would be served by re-membering your connection to the natural world.

There are lifetimes and eons in what we call "nature," and they can teach us how to see ourselves in our wholeness, to see ourselves as *seamless with*. Imagine having at one's fingertips not just plastic keys and electronic components, but an entire and infinite storehouse of material, inspiration, honesty, and beauty from which to draw for writing; nature is all of those and more. It provides fodder for written content as well as inspiration. The natural world brings us to our knees in supplication and buoys us up so we can be truthful.

As I was typing those paragraphs just above, I heard an incredibly loud thump and saw a flash of bright yellow in my peripheral vision; the lemon that seemed to me to suddenly drop off the branch had spent its entire existence as a fruit preparing for the moment when it would somehow loosen itself from its limb and become the pulp in my ice water. And please do not mistake that for consciousness in the limited way that we humans conceive of being aware; the lemon probably was not thinking *Oh, I will fall now and Writer over there will pick me up, slice through my middle, and masticate me in her water gulp*. However, there is a consciousness that is much larger than we can manage with our puny brains; it requires a dose of faith and a willingness to be called "silly." It is precisely this indefinable and infinitely complex consciousness that we can dip into if we align ourselves with the natural world around us.

Touching the blades of grass, lying face down in the stretch of lawn that lines two edges of my yard, I inhale. I settle into. I reconnect with something more eternal, more enduring, more perfect, more knowledgeable than any human can fathom. It requires willingness. Openness. A putting aside of the fear (of being called "ridiculous," of failing, of an ant crawling on my face as I lie with cheeks resting on grass, nose a bit deeper in mud).

Thus, I brought my computer outside this morning so I could see how it feels, what it is like to type on plastic keys that I really do not feel underneath my fingertips because I am listening to the world of nature around me, and thinking about how I am interconnected with all beings. I am not the only one interconnected, either. Do you remember that you are too? We are apt to forget. The adornments, material goods, fears *du jour*, and obligations sometimes keep humans in a state of disconnection and denial.

But I will write on this page and defend to the very last moment, this conviction—a mere faith, perhaps—that writing from our nature is what will save us. Because the natural world has death and shadow, the bleak black dark night of winter, and deserts of blazing heat. This is all part of who we are. A writer has nothing to lose by trying something new, especially if she is stuck, bored, grumpy, or confused in her writing pursuit. A writer has nothing to lose by pretending as if the natural world is a vast and unflinching treasure trove of memory, reverie, surprises-in-the-moment, and the very thing that holds us as we breathe, grow food, stand upon, or otherwise survive from day to day. Without this earth we would have no ground to stand upon; I mean this very literally.

I also mean it very literally for our writing: outer nature (stones, a crow, the sea) takes us along the journey of writing, abides near us, feeds us, and soothes us.

For the Doubting Thomases among us, I recommend going outside right now. No, do no wait until the wind settles down or the rain stops falling. Do not hope the blazing humidity will cool off later, or tomorrow, or in three months. The worry that you will interrupt your schedule for the day can be banished. For nature has the ability to sink us into the moment in some miraculous way that offers us hope. Rest. Release. The leaves that fall in slow motion in autumn, creating a collage of crimson and gold on the soil, will give any writer exactly what he needs in that moment to move forward, to dive deep, to crawl in hesitating fear or a faint, and right back into the settling of himself. And this will settle him into the writing task. It is a promise, so long as a writer goes willingly and openly. Even if she has a grudge in her step and a cramp in her jaw—actually, *especially* if she does—she would improve herself and her writing by walking toward the door to outside.

Do not waste one more minute. Go out that door now. Put this book down, step away from where you are sitting reading this passage. Let whatever doubt or fear is present—that voice telling you it's stupid or a waste of time—just chatter away in your head. Allow it to sit on your shoulder as you wander into the wide, wide world of wonder that patiently waits surrounding your home with the very life breath that keeps your lungs keeping you. Stand or sit. Lie down and allow the soil to soil you. For dirt is not the bad thing we were taught it to be as children. Dirt is what carries us, holds us, and—probably—prays for us.

A mockingbird has just sung a song from the top of the telephone pole as I sit here outside typing. She is likely the very bird who rustled the bush outside my office window in late spring. The one who wove a sumptuous nest in that bush and laid four crystal blue eggs in it. The bird who repeatedly darted at my head as I photographed her newborn hatchlings; the one who keenly eyed me from a high perch until I got too close to the chicks, and then compulsively swooped down with maternal protection and brushed the side of my face with her wing to say: *Leave my babies alone!* If that one small moment—unmeasurable in the increments we call "time"—can provide me with pages and pages of material for my writing, imagine what the whole of the nonhuman world can do for us writers! The truth is that I received the gifts of several weeks of blog entries, a newsletter section, numerous emails, and many journal entries of written material from that one bird's instinctual and brief act. I know that there was much more in that moment I could have tapped for my writing, perhaps volumes' worth.

It does not have to be the natural world, or birds, or human nature that is the *content* of a writer's project; if she just allows nature to be the locus of her *inspiration* she will have gone miles toward reconnecting with the very source that motivates, supports, calms, and blesses her. We do not deny who we are by going outside, although we might divert from that which keeps us in bondage to our small selves: worry that our hair will get mussed, our trouser cuffs dirty, our VIP schedule off track for the day.

My goodness, Writer! Feel the wind in your hair. See what color the dirt in your yard is as you toss the soiled-cuff pants into the washing machine. Explore what gems you can derive from shifting your calendar by ten minutes or so. And if ten minutes outside turns into three hours, count every one of your blessings that you are able to breathe and that the earth gives you that gift.

Words and Land Coming Together

We do the best we can with words. Writing is made possible by icons that we call, in English, "alphabet letters." We string them together into "words" that represent things, ideas, feelings, actions ... We strive to make these words live, to breathe something real onto the page. We reach deep down within us (to our guts for emotions) or impossibly high into our skulls (for concepts) in search of the conveyance (words) that will transport these things from our inner landscape to the outer one: the long white page.

*   *   *

There is an actual, tangible, natural wilderness out in the world. It comes to most of us in the "developed" world constantly in the streams of news, and usually in reference to global climate change worries. As we learn that these pristine, natural areas all over our planet are becoming smaller, scarcer, or less species-rich, we feel powerless. So many people who live with the types of built environments that include sidewalks have never had a true wilderness or outback experience. It is much easier to keep on moving through the landscapes that feel familiar, easy, comfortable ... in our own little status quo. And all the while we are numbing ourselves to the beauty and wisdom of the natural world; we are buffered from it. It's easier to be anesthetized with material ease than to actually feel the grief of these places.

And I do not write this out of blaring judgment but rather out of weepingly soft remorse and humility. Part of our humanity *is* this built environment in which we were raised and in which we raise our own children. But the error we make, some of us without even knowing it, is to mistake these buildings of metal, plastic, glass, plaster, even wood, as the entirety and fullness of our nature. We are oh-so-much more than that!

Many of us are so disconnected from actual wilderness lands that we scarcely know the meaning of "wild." A state park is not wilderness, nor is a wildlife refuge; we have touched so many corners and crannies of this fine, exquisite earth that we have forgotten what wilderness means. We are adrift in the human-touched, human-dominated world, and this has become what we conceive of as "normal." A little grassy lawn, a few planted

30

trees (native or not to the area), weekend hikes in the nearby trail system, and we feel we are connected to "nature."

But nature *as we conceive of it* (not even to mention "wilderness") is not a place full of raw inhibition but is, rather, a fenced, demarcated, mown, landscaped place that has been tidied into a human conception of nature. In fact, many of us have actually taken ourselves right out of what we define as "nature!"

Why not cultivate our inner wilderness as a way to move toward a rediscovery of the outer one? Why not allow writing to find us, to go in quest of our personal, unique—and yet universal—inner landscape: that very wild place within us that is untamed, primal, that roars a deafening and terrifying scream like the mountain lion on the far hillside? Writing can do this for humans; it takes a person straight into the depths of himself, into what is holy as well as profane—that raw, fecund part of a human that is inescapable. The tears that well up in our hearts (whether or not we allow them to spill over, out our eyelids, onto our cheeks, hopelessly rolling down the crevice edging our nose and clinging—salty, drenching, but cleansing and oceanic—to our lips) in the presence of fantastic beauty, or tragic loss, are our nature. Tears, and death, a sneeze, hair and nails that grow, lungs that take in air and expel by-products/waste, digestive and reproductive systems, our very need to eat and to drink water, lest we die: these are expressions of our very natural nature. And they make us more human than our cosmetics or house furnishings or vehicles. At least, the former are more likely to bring us closer to the irrevocable humanity we carry deep within. Homes and clothing come and go; we never cease needing to consume food and water. And the act of engaging the fullness of our humanity through writing brings us back to the centerpoint of who we are, the undeniable and inescapable fact of our existence.

The beauty of writing is that it does not have to be seen, at least not until the writer is ready. So a writer can feel free to pen his heart onto the page, to type his way to a deeper and fuller understanding of the glories of his life as a being rooted in the natural world. Because we are. Rooted.

*   *   *

Recently I have had the great pleasure of serving people who are finding their roots, their rootedness, their depth and dependence upon the life source, the life force that is not within our control but which animates us from conception to death. At least that long. These women and men have lost a fair bit of their *feeling* of connection to something bigger than themselves, something less explicable than the simple terms we come to describe and define ourselves: age, occupation, geographic location, family relations and the like. Please understand that *feeling* connected and *being* connected is one distinct landscape. We wrench them apart when we say we do not *feel* we are nature, or connected to it. Yet the very roots of our existence are always intact, at least as long as we have breath and a beating heart. So I work with these individuals to foster the part that is so easy to lose: the feeling of connection. They become aware, cognizant, conscious of the very life they live, and then they suddenly remember—as if waking from a dream—that life is significant just as it is right in this very place at this very time. Now. As we are.

This all concerns writing because one way to write is to move deeper into our rootedness. One way to move deeper into our rootedness is to write. It is a mutually beneficial relationship. Like commensalism in the natural world—each species living with one another without damage to either—writing lives off our rooted nature and our rooted nature lives off our writing. The simplest explanation for this is that when we take the time to get to know who we are by paring down our writing to the bare bones of our souls, and when we strip ourselves of our material possessions, we get to see who we really are.

One example is the woman I met who just so happens to be an underpaid ecologist in a truly-wilderness place on the planet. Her house, in fact her entire neighborhood, was destroyed in an uncontainable wildfire while she was out in the field conducting her research. Miraculously, her husband and children were spared, as were their pets. But they lived without a home for many months, sometimes sheltering their animals in a vehicle while they camped in the ashy rubble of what had been their backyard. When I asked about her experience of loss, she gave me a quizzical and silent stare. After a few long moments, she responded with: "I did not lose my human and canine family; that's all that matters." This woman had lost what most others would consider "everything" and yet she had the sum total of what really matters: her life and the lives of her loved ones. I have heard this story again and again in various contexts over several continents and a few decades. The roots of being human, and finding what remains to be a blessing worth honoring, is what I hope for each one of us. That we can be stripped of our tangibles just long enough to see that what we truly have and need are not those things that we can count. That we can strip down our writing so that bare essence of us can seep up—like a spring of crystal water in May—and fill our pages with truth, honesty, and soul.

I am not necessarily suggesting that an aspiring writer go out on a four-day-four-night wilderness fast alone in the desert. Although there are precious jewels to be found there, I realize that most people will not be open to this; it is too far a leap—too far in the opposite direction from how we live—to be a really viable choice for mainstream soulseeking. I am not suggesting that a writer move into the writing process with so few words that the lifeblood of the piece is lost in a sparse landscape of overgrown weeds and stale metaphor. Quite the contrary! I recommend that the compelled writer dash into the fullness of words, the flow and rushing tide that is the very voice of the heart.

When we let writing carry us away and when we immerse ourselves in the miracle of a single moment in the natural world (wilderness or not), we tap into something that transcends the material, the tangible, the trite. We find a depth to ourselves and to our writing that occupies the one distinct internal landscape: our inner wilderness. Allowing ourselves to become unfettered (e.g. by time, goods, responsibilities) and accountable only to that which resides in the depths of spontaneity and grace is where we find our writing souls.

*   *   *

I am walking in a forest healing from the ravages of a wildfire. On this day it mirrors a particularly burned out place in the landscape of my soul. Writing onto the page is an act of sheer compulsion and all begotten willpower unless I am rooted in the part of myself that remembers beauty in death, destruction and loss in transformation, fear in the calm of day. My body moves up the path, once a road, deeper toward the rock sharp mountains in the west. I see snow and a glacier up on the topmost peak, but down here the thick air is stagnant and breathes hot gasps onto my cheeks which now burn with shame. "Slowly" is my sole mantra, toward the burn site which holds within it the promise and hope amidst gray silty powder. As I move deeper into the site, my uncovered legs begin to darken with the ash. I can reverse-tattoo myself by putting a spit-wet fingertip onto my ashy skin; yet there is something deeply sacred, too, in just allowing my legs to become baptized in the residue of wildfire. I hear a spring but can only see a small seep running along the edge of the baby new grass that has to be this year's birth. The fire was last year.

As I move closer to the center of the small once-grove that not so long ago offered shade in the middle of this near-Death-Valley wild place, I feel my heart rate increasing, my heartbeat's powerful tenacity. It takes courage to see what lies in the middle of the burned out places of our inner wilderness. There are tiny drops of moisture forming in my eyebrows, along my upper lip, on the back of my bare-naked neck; it feels as much like nerves as my body's cooling response to the increasing noon heat. Each step is a labor and journey. Each few inches I mark as shoe prints on this dusty trail are leaves in a memory book of my history. When I finally reach the center, where I can see the charcoal black remains of what once lived, I feel a sudden ease wash over me. I realize that everything that lives, dies. I see that even after death, there is rebirth. And whatever I was worried about before I set out on this small walk is but a distant memory. I sit down atop the gray ash and pull out my journal. I write.

Chapter Three

OUR BODY AND THE LANDSCAPE OF FORESTED EARTH

This chapter explores our own physical body's relationship to writing, especially as we look at how it is sustained by the body of earth. The practices here include: exploring writing as a landscape, tangibly fostering connection with natural landscapes, and finding respite in comfortable outdoor spaces.

Forested Earth

Our body and the body of earth are totally interconnected. When we begin to experience the land on which we stand, we remember that connection. Very literally, we re-member ourselves as a part of nature. Like an arm or a leg is to our own body, so are we to the planet; when we are cut off from nature it is painful. We have become accustomed to the pain, even forgetting the origins of it. Instead, we imagine we feel discomfort from not having all that we want of material things, income, status, relationships, or whatever. But the truth, dear aspiring writer, is that the angst we feel is, at least in part, derived from the many ways we cut ourselves off from our real nature; said differently, we *are* nature.

We have a memory of being a child playing outside. The way we explore, connect, and find comfort on earth is through our body. The simple act of placing our hands on grass can be enough to trigger our memory as human, as *of the earth*—not separate from it. We seek comfort outside of us by going back to our roots, for example, to the base of a tree. We rest in its cradle and know we are not alone. We find how the knotholes of the tree are not so different from the hurt places in us: places where a branch fell off or something decayed is similar to life transitions and losses we face as humans. We realize, too, that the beauty of the canopy overhead is just like the respite we offer others with our smile.

Our Body's Relationship to Writing

The simple act of exploring the landscape of a page with a pen in our hands also connects us—our body—to writing. Like running in a field, our fast-moving pen catches the broad strokes of what is inside us: in our "inner landscape." Writing quickly helps us avoid thinking too much. It keeps us going across the page one word right after another, down the page one line to the next. We begin to lose our filters and lower our resistance: those things that kept us from writing in the first place. We allow whatever we find on the page to just be there. We write for the sheer beauty and movement of doing so; there is no deadline or prescribed outcome.

It is so obvious that we need our bodies for writing. Our hands and fingers holding a pen or moving across the keyboard are the means by which the words move between our brains and the waiting page. A writer might even be aware of how his shoulders hunch as he bends forward in concentration. Another feels the position of her feet and legs, bent in supplication to the writing process. Somebody else feels the hunger in her belly or the tightening of muscles. Few of us remember to consider our breath while we write. Few of us remember that it is exercise and food that keep us strong and flexible enough to write. Even the quiet sigh or whispered-aloud phrase from our scribing sometimes escapes our notice. But there is so much more that matters in writing than these commonsense relationships.

The body, our whole entire body, is in service to the writing process and project. It informs our writing; it instructs our writing. It bows down to and rises up from our writing in so many large and small ways. When we are ill or tired, fidgety or overfed—we can feel this in the writing. We can see how it detracts from the very good thing we are being called to write.

Essay: The Wide Landscape

Standing on the land, outside in the vastness of fresh air and birdsong, I feel the horizon stretch out from west to east. Even my peripheral vision, taking in a bit more than my focused eyes can hold, knows there is more. The landscape stretches out broadly to the left, to the right. It seems like it never ends. It is wide and stunning. It is as deep to each side as it is into the distance in front of me, perhaps even deeper. My mind knows that the sun will rise up over there and go down on the opposite side. But my heart feels the truth: that it is really circular, a spinning revolution. With my feet planted on terra firma, my heart roots into itself, into the whole of humanity. And beyond that to the whole of all that breathes, all that moves, all that walks, and swims, and flies. Even the apparently stationary beings—rocks, trees, ridge top—live, move, and breathe all in their own time and in their own way. My eyes and imagination can hold this knowledge, but the side-to-side width of land remains phenomenal; it carries the presence of all that is, the promise of all that will be, the deep memory of all that ever was.

So, too, the sheet of paper must be stretched out … from west to east. It is wider than it is long; it is in landscape orientation. I wonder if this was coincidence: my ability to write more deeply and more honestly with the page turned to landscape. This was not how I was taught to write "the important papers"; by junior high school the paper was oriented so that the student wrote from left to write within the 8½-inch space. But writing with the paper turned ninety degrees is how I have learned to write my soul, my heart. Most importantly, it is how I have learned to write my own human nature onto the page. As a young girl, I learned to draw, to color with crayons and paint, and then to craft individual alphabet letters on the page—using a dotted middle horizon line with a lower "ground" line and upper "sky" line, curiously manufactured in sky blue printer's ink on the paper—turned to landscape orientation. I strongly urge the aspiring writer to do the same with all journaling or any handwritten documents.

*   *   *

Rocking and rolling on a ship in high seas, motion sickness prevention medicine slightly blurring my usually sharp thinking, I sat staring out at the inky black waves of the Southern Ocean. Petrels and albatrosses graced the strong wind, their large bodies soaring, dipping: a dance like no other I had seen. Open in my lap was my travel journal. The pen lay inert on the paper, except when the heaving vessel tossed a bit out of sync with the wave patterns and the pen would roll to the other side of the nearly-empty, stark, white page. That ivory-colored page blared in huge color contrast with the water upon which we motored. A few more minutes of this heavenly meditation-on-water and I was ready to write.

My thick blue ink began to flow, glide, swim across the page, every word an expression of ecstasy at the novelty of this trip. Very few people have the privilege of going to Antarctica, the final wild frontier of this planet: owned by no country, isolated, windy, cold, dry, icebergs the only companion on the sea—but only once we got within dozens of miles of land. Otherwise, it was the petrels, albatrosses, and a few other seabirds that joined us across that long, incredible, and sometimes violent corridor: the Drake Passage. The pen I held seemed to capture my delirious delight at the prospect of being aboard ship for several weeks, away from work, away from responsibilities as simple as cooking my own meals and making my bed, away from all the land and earthscent and flora and fauna with which I was familiar.

And all this inched its way along my once-clean page, hopes and dreams walking onto the leaves of my journal, even the incoherence and inability to articulate these incredible new scenes onto a page that only understood words such as "woods, island beach, grassy yard." My page could take it all in though, even words that were grossly insufficient to the task at hand: making sense of the most impossibly novel outdoor landscape, seascape, I had ever seen. I had no way of understanding the size of petrels or albatrosses despite the field guide's precise description and measurements. How could I understand the twelve-foot wingspan against a sea larger and darker and more roiling than anything I had previously known?

But the landscape-oriented page knew, though consciously I did not. It took the other passengers, nosing about my chair and looking down at my page, who noticed and then remarked to me about the page upon which I wrote. *You have it turned "sideways, backwards, the wrong way," "How do you do that?" and "Why?"* It wasn't until these strangers commented on my freestyle writing—these people unfamiliar with journaling—that

I saw it as anything other than "natural." For at some point in the year prior, during my daily forays into the land of stream of consciousness writing—journaling for healing, journaling for the sake of my life and the lives of those around me—I noticed that my notebook had turned itself to landscape orientation. At first it surprised me. At first I chalked it up to being able to write more, faster, by having fewer shifts of my arm down to the next line. But then I began to see that the writing really flowed. My life really flowed. Everything just flowed onto those landscape pages.

How often do we see things move from top to bottom, vertically moving in the landscape around us? A shooting star will sometimes appear to drop from a "higher" position to a "lower" one in the sky, seabirds dive down to the shore or water's edge, rain and snow and hail "fall," suns and moons "rise" and "set," seemingly moving upward or downward. But most of the action, the movement in the landscape, is horizontal. Winds shiver trees so that boughs appear to move east to west, or west to east, or simply quiver all over with the delight of the unseeable power. Living creatures scurry, hop, or run—deer or rabbits, raccoons or ants—in patterns of right to left, left to right. We are rooted to this earth by the gravity of our lives, of physics; because of this, we are especially attuned to the left to right, right to left procession of beings.

Write and see for yourself with your paper in landscape orientation. Have available at least one back up ink pen. Because to stifle the flow with a pen that runs dry on a page turned to landscape orientation—and a heart full of words, stories, emotions, spiritual insights that just cry out to be scribed into the world—is to squelch the divine, indeed.

When the length of the paper is stretched out left to right, it is rooted, grounded in earth, grounded in ground. There is more of it to rest on the horizon of the earth. More of it to feel: like my smallest toes, the outer and inner edges of my feet, the ball under my big toe, the heel; it is all pressed down, feeling secure and naturally as it was designed: one with Earth. Like the beings who scatter themselves across a vast plateau of horizontal orientation, so too, our words will inhabit the page-turned-horizon. The words are to move quickly like scampering squirrels with cheeks full of the pine nut bounty, or coyotes dashing just because they can, or the lone horse at pasture who gallops freely through tall grass apparently for the sheer pleasure of it.

Writing the page horizontal is not an outcome-based strategy. It is a commitment to flow, to surrender to the unexpected, to live in the moment of freedom from knowing. Moving the pen without ceasing can be as lofty a goal as deliberate, thought-pondered sentences. For the latter leads to outcome-based writing, which ultimately has a purpose and goal of its own: project completion. But for now, just for these few minutes, allow the former to lead you deeper within, to the core, to the fine filament that connects all beings. To spirit. My encouragement is that you run across the landscape of the page, as uninhibited as the creatures who seemingly bound without a goal. We are not wolves in pursuit of prey. We are gazelles jumping and leaping, bounding and bouncing.

There is a kind of frivolity in stream of consciousness writing that loosens the usual patterns of writing, that is, writing based in thinking. Thinking has its place in good writing and toward a written outcome, of course (and I address this more fully later in the book). The genre into which the final writing project situates itself (academic paper, memoir, curriculum vitae, novel) is somewhat static, fixed, predetermined. But a landscape-page free-write is the foundational tool for moving forward with the *process* of writing. It is not outcome-driven, although the outcome will be derived from it. It is not goal-oriented, although the point is to further the goal. What I am conveying here is that the writing project (the outcome for which a writer sets out on the journey of words-to-paper) is not devoid of thought; but contrary to much of what we have been taught in grade school, must necessarily also incorporate the heart's wisdom. We do not get to soul through our heads. We do not reach tranquility and honesty through academic rigor.

But for the aspiring writer who feels immobile in the task, "landscape streaming" is powerful, evocative, honest, and surprising. Some of the best—that is, most inspired—writing comes from the unexpected process of showing up to the page open, willing, unassuming, and without judgment.

So the landscape journaling exercise becomes even more important for you because this is where you take a break, when you get to write whatever you feel like writing. Gifts and insights will reveal themselves when your head takes a break and lets your hand move easily, especially if it is moving quickly. These gems will enhance the work that comes later. For now, it's really important for you to just *be* in the exercise of landscape writing, doing it quickly and without thinking. The point of the journaling is not to generate content for your written project; we are not striving to identify the creatures who move in this biome, or to know which plants grow here. We are simply explorers, feeling the landscape around us—poking into dark corners, peeking under bushes, stretching ourselves out on a rock slab in the hot sun and watching the hawk circle overhead. Simply attending. Being. To enjoy the surroundings and goings-on on the landscape is not to deliberate. It is to observe, to see what happens, to be present without critique. So, too, is the journaling on the landscape.

We do not write wholly or fully or with the best writing outcome when we sacrifice process in the name of outcome. For outcome is only fully fleshed out, the actual animal breathing on the earth, when the heart is pumping blood through the corpus. Otherwise it is just a body, perhaps even beautiful and intact, but inert without the flowing lifeblood. And this flow is achievable when we give permission to the muse (the soul, the unexpected, the playful—even) to show up in our journals. This landscape-writing journey grows the writer into a full, flesh and blood, breathing entity, and in so doing grows the writing. In other words, the *writing* of the writer breathes and is given life through unencumbered, random, unpredictable scrawling of pen on paper.

The writing that appears on the landscape, on the horizontal page, does not care about perfection, tidiness, coherence, logic, function, or outcome. Again, this is not an avoidance of a tight, clear, beautiful writing outcome; there is nothing to balk at in a thoughtfully rigorous thesis, a cleanly composed résumé, a well-crafted memoir, or a compelling novella. But the fullness of self and project can completely elude the stuck writer who does not invite the inspiration (literally, *the breathing in of divine influence or divine quality*) of the open landscape page.

This is my strongest urging: the writer must allow herself the freedom to not know sometimes, to swim through the unknown just for the sheer experience of it. Sometimes the tides are strong and scary but the truth can emerge when we confront with direct freshness that which we do not know. Allow the knowing to come as a welcome guest—I mean, the heart's knowing. The head will always be there to cajole, to critique, to manage, and to perfect. But the heart will give the juice and life that every writer aspires to achieve. Even the most methodical, intellectual, "dry" (to those not impassioned with scholarly fervor) academic pursuit holds the hope of inspiring the reader. It is not just about informing ... not to the writer, anyway. But that which is imbued with the rigor of the heart is that which will widely reach those who might not otherwise find compelling the passions we each carry. That is, we do not inspire others with our heads; we do so with the wisdom of our hearts.

So go ahead. Move into the landscape, pen on page, and wander. Roam. Leap. Hop, skip, jump. Crawl. Meander. Walk backwards. Cry or giggle along the way. It doesn't have to make sense. Just cut a wide and wandering swath through the landscape of yourself. Note every bit that is in your field of experience, let everything come, and write it with a flourish. Write without care of form, function, mechanics, grammar, or even spelling. The guts of soul, the very nature of Nature, is within each one of us. We *are* Nature. And like the storms or sudden winds, there is no telling where the landscape will take the writer. Let east and west, the light and darkness, be your guides. Ramble. But always let the movement continue.

Landscape Stream of Consciousness Practice

Here's how to proceed. Find a page that is, at minimum, 8½ x 11 inches: standard computer printing paper size. The paper must be blank, absolutely and completely unlined. Reused paper is fine, as long as the print on the other side is not a distraction, does not detract from, the writing that must proceed from your heart. The pages can be loose leaf or bound. Handmade or manufactured. Expensive and ornate. Cheap and simple. For it is the words that fill it that will make it into something for you, the writer.

If necessary, set a timer for fifteen or twenty minutes. Resolve to journey across the landscape of writing for the entirety of that time. Pay no attention to watches or clocks. The very life of one's writing depends upon the progression through the landscape. For I know that there is no limit to the potential that awaits there. The fodder for writing from the wellspring of our deepest knowing (the heart's wisdom) does not run out. As long as we go to the land, seek out the raw and nonjudgmental experience of walking east to west, west to east, to the north and from it to the south, the writing potential will remain intact, vibrant and will—most assuredly—give its offering. We do not run out of things to write about when we are connected to the land. Because there is infinite, abiding, geologic-time expansiveness out there, and in here (I'm pointing to my heart). So our timepieces are irrelevant. But because so many of us live in the world of deadlines, time commitments, schedules—and the infernal need to fit our lives into the boxes on a calendar—allow yourself to be relieved of the ticking. Let the timer do its job. And in the space between hitting the start button and hearing the chime that signals the free-write is over, loose your body into the earth and ramble until the words sing their way onto the virgin white paper.

Seek, also, solitude. The exercise is not complete, fully colored with random beauty, unless you are alone, quiet, undistracted by the goings-on of others. Find a spot in the landscape of yard, home, park, that is a lonely one. For only in solitude, in loneliness, without phones or doorbells or others' chitter-chatter can the voices of the earth speak deeply and clearly to a writer.

This practice is not about editing. I ask anyone who dares to commit to this practice to avoid making changes as you write. Do not stop to look up the spelling of a word. Do not cross out a word you "mistakenly" wrote. Do not check for grammar or "logical" flow. These defeat the purpose of this exercise. The real surprises come when we think we have miswritten something. I have often found that a word I thought I had written in error actually became a touchstone for insight and clarity. Remember, the sole purpose of this practice is to get your hand moving across the page; it is our soul purpose.

Nobody else is going to see this writing so you can feel free to release whatever demons or angels live within you. If you tend to be a crusty soul, grumpy with the world, nobody will know that you become soft as a kitten as you scribble your vulnerabilities across the paper. If you tend to be timid in public, allow yourself to roar the cougar's fearless words in your private journaling practice. If you cannot write a coherent sentence or you use the same word fifteen times in fifteen minutes, do not worry. This practice allows you to unencumber yourself of whatever has built up over time. It might look very messy and scrambled and glaringly honest. Great!

Landscape Stream of Consciousness:

1. Go someplace you can be alone.
2. Turn off all sound: music, phone, television, radio, computer, iPod, or anything else.
3. Get several sheets of 8½ x11 unlined paper and a few pens.
4. Turn the paper to landscape orientation.
5. Set a timer that will alert you when fifteen minutes have elapsed.
6. Move the pen quickly across the page without stopping.
7. Do not change anything as you write.
8. Do not read what you are writing as you write it.
9. Allow whatever comes onto the page to remain there.
10. If you find your pen slowing down or you think you don't know what to write next, repeat the last words you wrote over and over until the next words come.

The Gentler Practice:

1. Follow #s 1-4 in the Landscape Stream of Consciousness practice above.
2. Write one sentence that comes to mind.
3. Pause.
4. Write another sentence that comes to mind, immediately followed by a second one that you might not have thought of before writing it.
5. Now write as many sentences as you can.

The Deeper Practice:

1. Follow #s 1-4 in the Landscape Stream of Consciousness practice.
2. Set a timer for thirty minutes.
3. Follow #s 6-10 above.
4. Make a commitment to doing this practice every day this week.
5. Renew that commitment one week from now.

Essay: Hands on the Earth

Every day for more than four years, I have placed my hands on the earth with intention. Yes, *daily*. It serves as my connection point between memory and tangible body, between the cultural amnesia about our oneness with landscapes and the actions that only my body can help me animate. Placing my palms on the surface of the grass or dirt, rocks, sand, hay, tree trunk, pond water, saltwater reminds me that my tears did not begin in my eyes or even in the fluid that is contained within me. They began inside my own human mother, and for all time turned backward from the very depths of the earth's salty oceans ... and perhaps before that, from stardust.

When I take the few moments to just pause in my workday, I begin the process of becoming humble. Humble enough to know that my work is not the linchpin upon which all things rely. Humble enough to remember that everything breathes and rests. And when I go outside, away from the computer, into the land of flying and crawling beings, I am made humble again. I re-member myself as one being out of trillions on this earth: one *Homo sapiens* out of seven billion humans on this earth, one medium-sized woman out of six and a half million species on land and over two million more in oceans.

When I place my hands on the dirt, I feel those who live in soil moving under my fingers and I notice the ant who crawls up my arm. I actually see how many blades of grass there are—even in a drought with thin, sparse strands of tan, dried up hay: more than I can count. I notice the fallen leaves—and in spring and summer, the leaves on the trees overhead. It is to the pebbles, sand grains, and dirt clods that I bow down in humility. It is underneath the broad canopy of daylight, or shining stars—an inconceivable expanse of ever-shifting beauty at a distance that my mind cannot fathom—that I recall how small, simple, and equal I am to all that is, and ever was, and ever shall be.

We are not separate from this earth, this land, this planet. We are not disconnected from the trees or that bird who just landed on the nearly bare winter cherry tree. Just as the soil receives nourishment from the rain, so do we receive from the earth nourishment for our body, emotions, spirit, and mind. Many of us have forgotten how much we depend on the land.

We have forgotten how to feel our closeness with nonhuman living beings, or why it matters that we do so. We have become utterly focused on how we are unique and different and more conscious than (so many think) the other living entities with whom we share this earth orb.

We need this re-membering, the act of tangibly reconnecting with the earth; by making physical contact every day, our memory becomes restored. We recall that the earth is a body too. We see how she restores herself season by season, how the birds continue to build nests, and the nurse logs continue to suckle those supple saplings that find their roots deepening into the fallen tree. It is this restoration of memory about our true nature that will save us. It will save us from the strife of working so hard to disconnect by donning cosmetics and purchasing an overabundance of non-essentials. It will save us from our cultural embarrassments regarding those bodily functions which are variably considered "inappropriate" and, instead, put them on a par with coyote scat and a skunk's mercaptans.

So I have created this everyday practice of putting my bare hands on the earth.

Hands on the Earth Practice

Find an outdoor space that you can visit daily. Be sure it is accessible to your home—the backyard, a river within walking distance, a favorite tree on your way home from work. Show up to that place with bare-naked hands. (If it is wintertime, take off your gloves or mittens.) Show up regularly, every day, no matter what. Begin with what feels comfortable enough. Perhaps you see a favorite flower or a familiar bush. Maybe all of a sudden you have a faint memory of being a child with grass blades between your fingers. Very gently place your hands upon the surface of this other living being. Open your palms wide. Unclench your fisted fingers. If you begin to feel afraid of how the surface will feel (too cold, too wet, too muddy, too sharp), see if you can focus on how it *actually* feels. Turn off the thoughts about this thing and close your eyes. Focus on what your fingers and palms are receiving. Notice which sensations surprise you or feel good. If you have immersed your hands in an icy stream that is now beginning to feel a bit like fire, or your fingers are throbbing, see if you can stay there for one … two … three more seconds before pulling your hands out of, or off, the surface.

Notice what is familiar, what is different, how you are the same as this living being. Over time, place your palms on different living beings. Maintain the physical contact with this earthy being by letting your hands get to know various surfaces, textures, entities, and by making a regular (I suggest daily) practice of placing your hands on whatever in the natural world draws you in. For each moment you spend, your body will begin to re-know its place in the natural scheme of all living beings.

What is it that you see and feel around you as you lay your splayed hands, your outstretched palms, upon the ground? Pretty soon your knees will bend and kneel on the ground. You may even feel like lying outstretched on the grass or in the dirt. How can you more deeply hear the wind's song in your heart? Or in what ways can you explore how the depths of your *inner* landscape feels as you connect with the pebbles of the beach under your hands, under your knuckles? In what ways does the dirt, the very soil, the mud, resemble your own skin?

As you become more familiar and comfortable with this practice, allow other body parts to make contact with the living natural world. Place your cheek against the silky surface of rose petals. Run your forefinger gently along the spines on its stem. Sniff a leaf; massage some rosemary, sage, or mint between your fingers; chew a fiddlehead; close your eyes and upturn your face to the snow or rain. Consider different postures, too. Get on your hands and knees in supplication to this great earth that holds us throughout our lifetime. Do yoga's child pose right there in the dirt, grass, or on the sandy beach. Lie prostrate on the ground. None of these are so far removed from our childhoods of barehanded mud pies, finger-sculpted sand castles, rolling down grassy hills, or flailing our arms and legs to make snow angels. Yes, this practice just might stretch how you think of yourself as a grown adult. But it also allows us to really embody the earth, to wear it as we were born to do. And as we knew how to do when we were young children.

You might need to banish a few voices from your head as you learn to become comfortable in this practice. *Dirty hands are bad. Wet clothes will make you sick. It's a waste of time. Only bohemians believe we are part of nature.* If you are plagued with thoughts such as these—or any others that curb your enjoyment and inclination to step outside the four walls of your built home—allow yourself to do it anyway. The thoughts will be there, or subside, or return, but they are not *you*. They are just thoughts.

Our hands feel the pulsing, breathing earth only after repeated connections with land. Like our relationships with other people, we must develop our connection to the land. Only for those of us who have fostered, nurtured, fed ourselves in nature, and worked to establish a relationship of companionship and equality with nonhuman beings, do we find the shared commonalities a natural response to placing our hands on the bodies of Earth.

I wonder what makes us think that we can write without our bodies. We need our hands, our eyes, our arms, our lungs. We also need the body of the earth. Have a relationship with it. What is your relationship to your body? What is your relationship to your heart right now? To your feet? Our lungs, the lungs of the trees, are part of the same body. To write in fullness, and wholeness, we need to be as connected to the earth as we can be. It is a nurtured relationship. It is make-believe to pretend that we can do without it.

Hands on the Earth:

1. Find an outdoor location you can easily get to from your house.
2. Visit daily.
3. Gently place your bare, open palms on something living there.
4. Notice sensations.
5. Feel what is the same in you and on the earth.
6. Stay there for a while.

The Gentler Practice:

1. Find one living thing just outside your door (a plant, tree, flower).
2. Look at it everyday at about the same time of day.
3. On the third or fourth day, decide which part of the living being feels comfortable (safe) to you.
4. Gently touch that part of the living being.

The Deeper Practice:

1. Follow #s 1-2 in the Hands on the Earth practice.
2. Plunge your hands into the mud, a pile of leaves, a leafy bush.
3. Get as much of your body in contact with this surface or being.
4. Rub the leaves or mud or flowers of this being.
5. Hang out there for a long while.
6. Make a commitment to engage this deeper practice at least weekly, with the basic Hands on the Earth practice as your daily ritual.

Essay: Earth As Hearth

A hearth is not just a fireside; it is a sanctuary representing home and safety. A hearth is a haven for many of us. So is the actual body of the earth. The trees dance for us as a greeting. The ocean waves thump their reminders of the ongoing cycles that hold this planet intact. The winter snows blanket the land in silence and wonder. The very soil under our bare feet can offer us a ground onto which we let loose our tears without fear of judgment or correction by our human fellows.

Like gathering around a fire that gives us a cozy place indoors, the natural world outside four walls can also provide for our needs of safety and coziness. Climbing onto the wide branch of an oak, burying ourselves in sand, hiding behind a bush: our younger selves might have been privileged to live in a place that offered such explorations and comforts. The farther we were raised from natural places—the more we only knew the safety tucked in under a roof and walls—the less we might be inclined to think about nature as a refuge.

But instinctively, we know. Because we are human, natural, of nature. Our feet stand rooted on the earth every day. Our bodies know how to mimic nature as we lift and stretch outward our arms. We know the sound of rain and the smell of a pine tree. Even if shoes and socks dampen our bare-skinned toes' connection with the soil and a raincoat keeps us from experiencing the tingle of raindrops on forearms, even if a wide brimmed hat keeps the sun off our noses—even then, we are nature and are connected via a lineage of roots and veins, the intake of air and the release of wastes. Nature can be a wonderful place of retreat, quiet contemplation, soothing the din of daily life, winding down our thoughts or emotions, becoming still.

Life happens and sometimes it is sad and lonely, or fear inciting, or very exhilarating. Writing can also evoke emotions. What I've learned about myself and my clients who are doing extensive writing projects— like writing a novel or a memoir—is that even the really exciting, happy, blissful emotions can hamper our writing. So thank goodness we have the ample, supportive mother of Earth to quietly receive whatever it is we need to let go. Some of us are not going to initially feel comfortable going out into the natural world for a calming experience. Many have lost the tender connection that affords a facile embrace of the beauty and support that the living nonhuman world has to offer. The practice I offer here is one that grows and deepens with repetition over time. The way we find solace, release the energy of excitement, slow down our anger is through a sense of connection and a relationship that is fostered, nurtured, embraced and finally sought-after. A relationship with the land.

Some of my favorite places are forests, as well as individual trees. (The name of my business intentionally includes the word "arbor.") Rainforests. The Joshua trees of the Mojave Desert. Ancient bristlecone pines. The ponderosa pines whose fragrant sap is still a touchstone back to my childhood summer days, the respite I'd find in their shade, lying on the thick needle beds at the base of their trunks on glaringly hot days. The maples and oaks in my relatives' humid, east coast yard. My grandpa's instructions about how to identify each tree's leaf shape. The alders that fall each year in the Pacific Northwest, shallow root bases that loosen their hold in windy winters. The red, soft, intriguing bottlebrush blossoms; the "poky ball" seeds of the liquidambar; or the slender, lavender, "milk"-releasing jacaranda flowers that my little girl self created stories about during long hours alone with these trees in my backyard. Too, the sycamore in the front yard of my childhood home whose roots cracked and displaced the cement walkway that needed to be smooth in order for my brother's wheelchair to safely pass; it was my sentinel outside my bedroom window until we had to have it cut down—an act which caused my strong mother to cry the only time that I can remember during my entire growing up years. The hardwood forests of New England, shockingly short in stature by my west coast standards, shockingly brilliant during my first east coast autumn.

I have ... hiked, walked, climbed, bushwhacked through; slept and crawled beside; cried, laughed hysterically, screamed and yelled under; worked, planted, uprooted, explored, identified, researched on behalf of; written stories, essays, about; painted and collaged and hugged and photographed; driven hundreds of miles to; jumped from the tops of; given speeches about ... many different species of trees and types of forests during my lifetime. It is no exaggeration to say that my bodily, emotional, intellectual, and spiritual life depends upon the existence of trees.

Earth as Hearth Practice

Explore the natural areas around your house. Find a forest, park, or a really large yard that is private. Find a treesy estuary or edge of a meadow near your home. Determine a location that is readily accessible and solitary. For every practice in this book, especially the earth-based ones, I strongly recommend that you do them alone, by yourself. I urge you to leave your cell phone at home, inside, or turned completely off. Leave your dog at home, too.

I want you to look for a few specific qualities in the location you are about to choose. First, find someplace where you can be totally alone, uninterrupted, and quiet. Next, find a location that feels good to you. It should be aesthetically pleasing, and would best serve you if you can feel even a little bit at home in this place. Finally, find a space that feels protected and protective to you. For example, is there a canopy overhang (such as a willow tree has) underneath which you can sit or lie down? At the edge of the beach, can you find a protected rock cove into which you can nestle? In your yard or a park, against which tree trunk might it be comfortable and cozy enough to lean?

Once you have found your haven, go there and stay for a while. Take note of what is beautiful and feels good about this place to you. Then notice what is dirty, broken, sawn, cut, mowed down, or fallen. Imagine how the place looked before it was littered, built-upon, cut down or pruned; see if you can reconstruct an image of lushness that makes it even more safe and beautiful to you.

Turn your attention to the way in which your back is supported by the tree trunk, or the way in which the rocks or bushes hide you from other humans. Notice how the land, trees, grasses continue on in their respiration, swaying, or stillness—apparently accepting and calm about all that you have to spill forth onto her skin. Remember how the seasons continue to cycle; how the flowers sprout, bloom, fade away; how the sun rises each morning and the moon moves from new to full over and over and over again.

The idea for this practice is to simply have fun, to enjoy the experience, to try something out of the ordinary for you now that you're an adult. Move through your area, exploring the details. See how the wind feels on your face as you sprint across the grove. Notice the richness of visual images: textures, light and shadow, the contrast between bark and leaves on a single tree. Climb up onto a tree branch and dangle your legs, swinging them in time to a song you recall from your youth. Etch a pattern into dirt or mud. Notice how the mushrooms all line up, tracing the dot-to-dot pattern. Imagine the forest as an actual home and see where you might decide to cook a meal, sleep, hang out, or take a bath. Collect stones or branches. Rake the leaves (or pine needles) into a pile with your outstretched arms; sit or lie down in the pile. Touch a rock that is exposed to the sun and feel its temperature on your skin; do the same with a rock that is in the cool shade.

I will write this again: the actual body of the earth is a sanctuary, representing home and safety. While you may not feel this in the first weeks of visiting your outdoor haven, allow yourself to suspend disbelief. Imagine that the natural features that comprise your outside hearth grew there with *you* in mind; take a step closer to the idea that perhaps a power greater than you knew your difficulties and created this special site uniquely for you. See how you can grow a friendly response to this place. Notice what begins to sprout over time in the rocks, bark, or grasses that hold your body as you visit this location repeatedly. And know, without a doubt, that even as your tears turn the soil of earth to mud, or your laughter is carried on the breath of the wind, so too will something withering sprout anew as you move your body to the writing page.

Earth as Hearth:

1. Locate a quiet natural area around your home where you can be alone.
2. Search for a specific place within this natural area that feels especially good to you.
   a. It should feel safe.
   b. It should be pleasing to you.
   c. It should be very comfortable.
   d. It should have some protection (overhang, plant or rock cover, large tree trunk).
3. Take time to simply notice what is around you—both the beauty and any brokenness.
4. Begin to move in this place—exploring and touching, trying out different positions.
5. As you move, see the small things of this place.
6. Over repeated visits, notice the tiny changes that occur.
7. Pay attention to the natural area, noticing how you are protected and supported by it.

The Gentler Practice:

1. Follow #s 1-4 in the Earth as Hearth practice.
2. Pay attention to the natural area, noticing how you are protected and supported by it.

The Deeper Practice:

1. Follow #s 1-7 in the Earth as Hearth practice.
2. Pay attention to how the land, plants, crawling creatures notice your presence and alter their behavior in response.
3. Identify one being or aspect of the natural area that feels most soothing. Imagine that this plant, creature, or thing cares about and supports you.

~€ Chapter Four €~

OUR EMOTIONS AND THE LANDSCAPE OF OCEAN WATERS

This chapter explores our emotions in relationship to writing, especially as we learn to write about and clarify the impact of emotions on our writing project and process; seeing how water flows on earth aids us as we experience the currents of our emotional landscapes. The practices here include: letting go of hindering emotions as we sit to write, becoming clearer about what we are feeling, and experiencing the ebb and flow of water.

Ocean Waters

We feel an inexplicable draw to a particular landscape. As we remember, we re-member: we sew ourselves back on to the body of earth becoming a conscious member, again, of who we are, from what we came, and to where we go when life passes away. The vast oceans carry some of the same life-giving stuff as our blood. They model for us how to ebb and flow.

Once we begin to remember the fullness of who we are, we also find that there are things we tried hard to forget, things we really did not want to remember at all. We come up against loss, fear, intimidation, demands, insecurity … demons of all sorts. Some of these are imposed from outside of us; others are imposed from somewhere deep and forgotten within us. All of them stand like guards preventing us from writing. Ignoring them only serves to strengthen their hold; we become blocked. We cannot erect all these barriers without being subject to them. I cannot expect that the fence I build in my yard will keep out intruders but still allow me free access; I must unlatch the gate to get through.

But accepting that these hindrances are there without catering to their demands—acknowledging that we all have these particular impediments but that we do not have to surrender our power to them—is a way through to our writing. Letting go of these voices *temporarily* can help us. We become clear about the negative messages we carry within us about our writing, and then we set them aside during our writing time. It is then that our writing begins to flow; it is only then that *we* begin to flow.

Our Emotions' Relationship to Writing

This section is intended for people who are actively engaged in life, with its varying shapes and hues of emotional engagement with self and others. This is especially for writers who need to emotionally recover from something that has happened or who are stuck, blocked, impeded. With a few simple practices (that we do over and over on a regular basis), we can find the freedom and spaciousness in our inner landscape to do the hard work of watering a garden of writing.

Emotions matter in writing. Sometimes they are the emotions associated with the content of what we are writing. Often—perhaps *more* often—the emotions that matter most to us when we're writing are the ones that we experience in the present moment. Sometimes we have emotions about relationships in our life. Sometimes we have emotions about the circumstances in our life. Sometimes we have emotions about the process of our life in any given moment. And sometimes we have emotions that connect us back to things in our past.

There are distinct ways in which the writer's emotional landscape stands as an impenetrable gate between herself and her writing. One way this becomes evident is when the content of what the writer is working on causes emotions that make writing more difficult. So many times writers have sat down to compose something—often it's a document which is compulsory, near its due date, or simply out of the range of possible interests of the writer—and felt sickeningly bored. How frequently this occurs! We are writing content about which we are not enthusiastic, or perhaps might have been enthusiastic had we more time before our deadline.

This gap between emotion and writing is perhaps manifest most widely in the daily trivia of living our lives. I know somebody who is ready to lose her job. She blames herself, and she blames the system from which she is being extricated so ungracefully. This single woman is frustrated and scared. In preparation for rejoining the workforce as a middle-aged woman, she is compiling her résumé and writing cover letters. But she is greatly stymied she is as she does so; high emotion is clashing with professionalism as she attempts to write her accomplishments and qualifications onto the page. Her inner landscape feels the intense sting of the current employer's rejection of those attributes. Until she moves through her emotions, she will continue to face difficulty in promoting herself.

We do not need to be in the middle of such a huge dilemma to be stifled in our writing. Other basic emotional events in our lives can also stand in the way of our writing: confrontations with a coworker, the requirement to conform to a particular style or type of writing we dislike, angst about how well we will achieve a particular outcome; these all create impediments to the easy flow of written pieces.

Essay: The Inner Critic

There is a voice that comes; this one is not friendly. It is a loud booming, grate-on-one's-nerves type of voice. We hear it in stereo reverberating on canyon walls, echoing down the valley, powerful enough to shiver the grasses. Sometimes it rocks the earth on which we stand; other times it simply rocks us back into our cradle of familiarity. Because, though it is a foe, the voice is a *familiar* familiar. And if there is anything at all that a writer wants during her writing time, it is something known to which she can cling with ferocity. She does this because writing is unsettling. It is easier to go to places we can find; what we encounter in the commonplace are all the voices that have ever offered us a way out, an escape. These voices are the ones that deliver the most unwanted and yet most expected news: that the writer is inept, incapable, has better things to do with his time. The voice feeds us with all the reasons that we are not up to the task of writing. In fact, we might as well not even try.

It resembles our own speech, for it is coming from within. It is our inner critic.

Perhaps the voice, or the jury—as it sometimes feels—is imbued with those old, ancient, witch-like ones that came to a young child just working through her first writing project. Perhaps it was a grade school paragraph, a high school term paper, or a college prep essay. Maybe that writing task came early, or arrived over and over again throughout one's youth. But always with it came the adult's words: "too much" or "too little" of something. In short, the writing lacked, was insufficient, deemed "wrong." And oh my, that little guy who hears that message once is in trouble enough; the one who is relentlessly told—and often with all the best intentions for his "improvement"—will learn to turn down the critique because it is too harsh, too loud, too overwhelming. The problem is that the emotional landscape is imprinted now with those messages: bent, burnt trees that can never be regrown. And so it goes for the child-turned-adult. The sounds she consciously "muted" became a fixture in her internal landscape. Even when she grows up strong and tall, standing rooted in her gifts, the writer carries those old echoes and they become primal screams just waiting to be released.

Those yells and criticisms and demeaning words that come from the depths within are not even telling the truth, or the whole truth, so help the writer! The words and scolding that the voices scare up from behind dark stones on the path are merely telling stories. Sure, the stories *sound* real. But they are just words, albeit deviously put together into judgments that could stop even the most intrepid in their tracks. Pronouncements. Declarations. Threats. Insults. Even ultimatums. The problem is that the voice is very cleverly seductive. Oh, so alluring. It tells us we are far better off without making the journey; home is safer. Staying stagnant will not hurt as much as moving.

That first unfamiliar place the writer must go when staring at the page waiting to be filled is to that place of new voices: one's own clear brightly ringing inner voice, for example. We have to discover our unique, authentic, more powerful voice: the one that speaks from our depths the calling to write. Now *that* is an honest story.

*   *   *

Trudging along weary and aching, the hiker has already forgotten the potent views at the top of the ridgeline. He feels that old knife-sharp pain in his knee, the burning feet with a blister well developed after the day's fifteen miles, the knot in his shoulder. The T-shirt he wears clings to him unnaturally, sweat moistened and dried repeatedly throughout the day. Each step is a hardship even though he is aided by gravity as he moves downhill. He will soon reach the waiting respite of the vehicle and the hot bath salts on the other end of the car ride. None of these things matter to him. In this moment, he is hurting. The writer can have this experience too; usually it is the inner landscape that is slogging along.

We have emotions. Anger, fear, sadness, confusion, grief, loneliness, apathy, and overexcitement are part of the landscape of daily life. Interactions occur, events happen, and we find ourselves reacting. This is normal. This is human. These can interfere with writing though, and in a very significant way sometimes, too. Many of the practices I offer in this book deal with aiding, nudging, and guiding the writer toward an emotional landscape that is conducive to writing. When emotions are strong, they can impede the writer, and skew the writing. This does not make the writer "bad," or the emotions "wrong." It shows that the writer is, indeed, fully engaged in life as a human being, and has the resulting diversity of emotions that accompany life's journey. We can use these to our advantage, as writers: our despair can be the way we relate to a character we are writing into our fiction. However, sometimes the emotions stand in our way: our despair can strip us of the energy we need to move forward with the difficult task of research on an academic project, for example.

There are myriad emotions, and multifarious ways in which they can stand tall, arrogant, defensive between us and our writing. Softening to them helps. But sometimes we get bowled over by the power of them and we simply cannot proceed. To focus, concentrate, muster the will or strength or courage to turn on the computer and open the document feels daunting. We couldn't imagine typing something onto that empty page staring us in the face, threatening like a monster with a club. Even the arduous downhill portion of the hiking adventure—with its promise of the return back to the comforts of home, the glory of the abidance with nature and memories of the sweeping views on the mountaintop, the relief and release from our daily obligations—can become drudgery and cast a cloud over the blessing of being out, and free. Sometimes—despite all the fortitude we conjure up and our outward patina of strength, conviction, and attendance to the writing—the frailty of our real condition, the actual emotions we feel but decide not to share, lurk threateningly within.

There is an entire and vast wardrobe of coverings that we employ to make it through the moment, the day, the workweek, and our lives. Some of these are truly costumes: even *we* don't believe that we are the character we dressed up as. But we wear them as a disguise, a way to pretend *as if* we are funny, wise, older or younger, serious, content, or calm. But the writer's writing knows different; it knows the truth.

As if a sentient being in and of itself, Writing understands the real inner landscape of the writer. Writing does not wear pretense or use facades. It can feel what is really going on with the writer and, at every turn, it betrays the writer's actual experience. If the writer sits down with hands on keyboard in a fit of despair, but expects to compose a section of the narrative that is singingly hopeful, chances are she will not be able to pull it off. Or, Writing will take over for the writer and perhaps move her to a place of hope by the time she releases herself from that session at the computer.

The writer must put aside the discordant chorus of voices. The committee, the panel, the demons. Perhaps because writing is such a solitary and quiet endeavor, those voices gain volume and momentum. And it is not long before the unsuspecting writer is faced again—for the umpteenth time—with the need to turn down the volume. But, these voices beg for attention. So we give them a little.

Scrap the Inner Critic Practice

The writer must take a few minutes to write down every single thing s/he is hearing. Until we become practiced at this, it might be challenging to tease out the words. Especially when so many disruptive messages are being hurled into the tiny ovoid space between our ears, making out the actual messages becomes the task. Also, we instantly want to deny those voices that seem true. The truer the critique in our heads, the less likely we are to actually hear it. Yes, it's odd that way. But sit anyway, pen poised across the blank, horizontally aligned, unlined page. It is permissible—and even something I encourage my clients to do—to write a few irritating words as the writing prompt at the top of the page. Take the most blatant message, the one that even you cannot deny, and scrawl it as your writing prompt across the upper left hand corner. Write it crookedly, just to tease it a bit. An effective sentence that works for a lot of aspiring writers (or even savvy, published ones) is, "You do not know enough (yet) to do this writing project." The real rub in this short sentence is that it gives the writer false hope: if she just does something— *any*thing—she will acquire (learn) what she needs in order to proceed with her project. It convinces the writer that there is something else valid and even crucial to the writing task. The trick is that it does not involve writing. The *only* way to write something is to actually put fingers on a keyboard or pen in hand moving across a page. I can assure any writer that there is no more research, no more fact-gathering, no more time, no more of anything that the writer must do to begin writing … except to actually put words onto the page.

Use that sentence above—or any other sentence or phrase that feels especially true, scary, and debilitating for you—and let that be the prompt you write when your hand wants to slow to a crawl and then to cease writing altogether. Spend ten minutes writing down all the ways in which you are insufficient, disturbed, undereducated, overemployed, emotionally exhausted, economically underprivileged; living in a house that is too dirty, too quiet or loud, too isolated; and around people who don't care, think you're silly, dislike your writing idea, and—in fact—how even *you* can't stand your writing idea.

All sorts of really important things will suddenly come to mind that need your attention: laundering—by hand—all the curtains in the house, dusting behind the utensils in the back of that drawer, refolding the towels so they look tidier in that dark closet, scheduling every medical appointment for the next three years—for *every* member of your extended family and perhaps for a few friends. Or, answering immediately that text message from your loved one who knows you are just sitting down to write and who has secretly conspired with your inner critic to keep you from doing so. You'll suddenly need to dump out that old tomato juice in the back of the fridge and, while you're at it, might as well go out to buy a bottle brush and scour the inside with hot soapy water so you can use it as a back up to the back up to the water bottles in the car. And those voices in your head will tell you that you must do this inane task right now, this instant. Because any other task besides writing can be a welcome diversion from giving the inner critic his turn on the page; it doesn't feel good and we don't like it.

So the inner critic's words get scribbled across page after page after page in your journal. For those ten minutes. Then stop. Look at what you wrote. Find the words (phrase or sentence) that feel the harshest, or which you've repeated the most in your free-write. If it's difficult to choose just one, then pick the three or four that really suck the life out of you—that knock the wind from your body and leave you panting on the hot pavement. Find a scrap of paper (best if it's dirty and a bit torn) and write that one (or three to four) obsessively distracting and excruciatingly mean phrase(s) on that unsightly ripped scrap of paper.

Now ... take that scrap and fold it up as small as you can. Or tear it into as many pieces of confetti as you are able. Burn it. Flush it down the toilet. Or, simply, sit on it as you write.

This simple but symbolic act has great power. I can assure you that this is not a therapy exercise that will suddenly free you of the demons that want to keep you from writing. It will not exorcise the manic tendency to avoid writing at all costs (most especially, at the cost of the writing project you aspire to). In other words, this is not a permanent "solution." But this exercise, especially if you repeat it every single time you sit down to write, will give the voices just enough attention that they feel acknowledged (which is, strangely, a temporary sedative for them) and allow you a few minutes of unencumbered writing time. It puts the thoughts on "pause" or "mute." For remember, these voices might have belonged to a real person (that fearful adult who did not honor your unique creativity when you were six years old), but now these thoughts are within each one of us. If we listen just carefully enough we will hear a bit of our own twang, speech impediment, or favorite slang words in the voices in our heads.

So it is a bit shortsighted, or perhaps overly idealistic, to imagine that one little practice will release us from, essentially, our own insecurities and fears about writing. But it can train us in the practice of taking a break from the voices, ignoring them for just a little while. And your tolerance will build up over time—especially as the goodies, the real juice from writing, become part of your landscape—so that the scrap of paper exercise will carry you through longer and longer spells of (relatively) critique-free, distraction-free writing time. This practice does not eradicate the voices as much as release their power: their long-nailed, finger-clenched grasp on our wrist. *Now* we can begin to shape our experience into words on a page. You can feel free to revisit the demons free-write or the scrap with mean mantras parts of this exercise as frequently as necessary to enable showing up to the page.

Scrap the Inner Critic:

1. Write down all the things you hear in your head about why you are not up to the task of writing.
2. Spend no more than ten minutes doing this.
3. Select one to several short, negative phrase(s) from the writing you just did.
4. Find a small scrap of paper.
5. Write the negative words you selected onto the scrap of paper.
6. Destroy the little scrap of paper.
7. Do this practice as many times as you need to before and during your writing session.

The Gentler Practice:

1. Get out a small torn or dirty scrap of paper.
2. On that piece of paper, write down one short sentence about how you feel stuck in your writing. (You could start the sentence with: "The hardest part about writing is _____.")
3. Tear up the piece of paper into tiny bits.
4. Start working on your writing project.

The Deeper Practice:

1. Follow #s 1-2 in the Scrap the Inner Critic practice.
2. Circle three short, negative phrases in the writing you just did.
3. Tear a piece of paper into three ragged scraps.
4. Write one negative phrase on each of the scraps.
5. Write a few more words on each scrap of paper, free associating other negative words that each phrase brings to mind.

6. Tear up each scrap, and place the pieces into a fireplace.
7. Light the bits on fire.
8. As the smoke rises and the paper burns, imagine your own negative thoughts going up in smoke.
9. When the small fire is extinguished, sit down immediately and begin to work on your writing.

Essay: Photographic Clarity

Slowly or quickly the writer moves through a particular project. Sometimes the process requires tedious snail paces, each word seemingly on the other side of the mountain. Sweat, uphill climbs, slippery sand the substrate on which the writer struggles for a foothold. Maybe it is more like a hot dune in the Sahara with teasing mirages and double effort in each sand-laden footstep. Perhaps the writer feels like he is preparing to race in a marathon: diet changes, cross-training, increasingly long practice runs, a schedule to follow to make the mark that will earn the runner the title "marathon runner." It does not matter what the speed of the writing looks like, how the writer is dressed, how hilly or flat, short or long-distance the writing goal. What matters most is clarity. How crystal clear and sparkling clean the message the writer wants to convey must be!

For the writer does not write in a vacuum, closed off and secreted away from society, from readers, from the eyes that will roam the page searching for meaning in another's words. Even if the writer goes on retreat, lives in a convent, or says how much she does not care that the world see her work, there is a part of ourselves that is begging to be heard—no matter how hard it is to admit. However soiled our experience, there are people "out there"—a whole waiting world, in fact—who need to read what we have written. There is no higher power in all the universes that ever banged into existence with one big blast who would cajole, entice, tantalize, or beseech a person to write unless there was a very good reason. A *very* good reason. And that purpose for writing—every writer's purpose, however honest or dishonest she is about admitting it—is to have somebody else place eyeballs upon page, heart upon intention, mind on idea, and receive whatever it is the writer has scribed.

The first person to do so is the writer herself. But she cannot be trusted to account accurately for all that needs to be read. Her sole endeavor is to write as honestly, as clearly, as deeply as she can muster so that her truth can be given away to her audience, her readers. Writing is the act of giving a gift. We all have offerings that the world needs. If a person is compelled to write, despite her own best desire, then she better get on with the task and do so with as much integrity as possible. For once the call has planted itself in the heart of the writer, as soon as he has turned that call into an idea that can be written down, he is hooked, he is obligated, he is bound by all the powers that be to do so, lest he reach the end of his life with the abiding sense of incompletion. (I know people for whom this was the case.) The writer will be the first to read her work but she will not be the first to *receive* it.

Reading and receiving are very different. The former is an act of cognition, of sensory stimulation. The latter is a heart thing. Yes, an act of the heart. How many times have we offered assistance to somebody who refuses our help! It is not the job of the writer to receive her own work. She is the conduit through which the writing flows, the instrument, the scribe, the put-into-words-er. And while she reads her work, and re-reads it, her job is to give the gift to the waiting reader. The only way to do this is to trust that we are offering something.

Clearness of purpose can come with a simple admission of hope: *I want to write this book. I will show up to the page until it is finished.* But the clearness of *message* is what this chapter is about. Clarity. Crystalline.

*   *   *

I had an amazing experience with the photograph practice (that follows) as I facilitated some writing activities for a small group of women who came to one of my workshops years ago. I had prepared some laminated prints of nature photographs I had taken with my digital camera. Some of the images were overly-magnified parts of animals (bird wing, fur, eye); others were severely blurred images that would have been recognizable had I focused properly. Still a few more had been angled and cropped so that even a clear image became hard to decipher. All of them looked like abstract paintings. I passed out more photographs than the number of participants in my group; I wanted everybody to have a choice of photos. The simple instruction was to pick the first photograph that either enticed or disenchanted them and to turn it face down in front of them until all of the participants had an image. About a third of the way through the selection and passing process, a woman chose a photograph with a grunt. I figured she had picked an image she really disliked.

I called the group to action once the last person chose her image. I asked these novice writers to do a free-write about the photograph in front of them, looking at the image as much or as little as they needed to during the writing process. At the end of the fifteen-minute activity, I asked them to drop their pens and lay their photograph on top of their page. We then debriefed; those who wished to share talked about their experience of this exercise: what they saw in the photograph, what it evoked for them, what they wrote about, where it led them as they journeyed through the free-write.

The woman who had shown displeasure at her photograph offered to share. Hers was one of the images I thought almost too literal for the exercise: it was a very up-close image of brown, black, and off-white tree trunks that had been burned in a fire. To me, it was very obviously birch tree trunks with scorch marks from a blazing hot fire. It never occurred to me that anybody would not see that in the image. (I did not tell the group what I had taken pictures of to create these photographs.) This woman began by telling the group that she had no idea what the image was but that it repulsed her so much that she was compelled to choose it. She then went on to describe how depleted she felt in her life, how much she had loved and lost in recent years. She said, "I feel so burned out." The woman then courageously read to the group from her free-write page. Everything she had written down included fire imagery, burnt items, smoke, and destruction. Her words were hauntingly beautiful and provided each of us with the most clear, detailed, and specific story about what she meant by "burned out."

Somehow the image this woman could not literally translate into something "knowable" in her mind (a tree that had been ravaged by fire) was translated into the language of her soul (a feeling of being burned out, wearied, by the hardships in her life). It was, indeed, a photograph that represented that part of her journey. She had those moments of inspiration as she did the free-write because she entered the clarity of the photograph and found mirrored within it her own difficult landscape of loss.

Photographic Clarity Practice

So now it is your turn. Pull out that horizontal, landscape-oriented journal. Have your pens ready—the starting pen and the backups. Choose a photograph of the most intangible, abstract image you can find. Perhaps you took a photograph that came out very blurry; that would be a good choice of images for this practice. Maybe there is a piece of abstract art pictured in one of your coffee table books or hanging on your wall; these would be suitable, too. Images of the natural world are ideal, especially those that are magnified to such an extent that the entirety of the object cannot be seen in the photograph. Another option would be a photograph of an animal or wild nature scene that is foreign to you, that depicts a scene into which you have never walked in waking life. If all you can find is a photograph with a clearly defined image, then you should rotate the image sideways or upside down; orient the photograph so that you are not viewing it as it was intended.

While deciding what image to use for this exercise, it is especially helpful to choose one that is particularly striking to you. Maybe it evokes awe and wonder. Perhaps you notice a smile half-formed on your face. Or, you might see a photograph and quickly turn the page as your revulsion rises like bile to the throat. Either one of these reactions to a photographic image is precisely what we are seeking for this writing exercise: magnetized attraction, absolute putrefaction.

Now, as quickly as the pen can move, note everything you can about the image in the photo. The writing can be a description of what shapes you see, or what color schemes emerge. It can be an accounting of every detail of the image. Too, you can free associate: if your pen notes the items as having the colors "red leaf and green stem" and the next thing you imagine is a Christmas decoration, then move forward into the writing with that holiday theme. The idea is to write as much as possible in five to ten minutes. If you have exhausted the ability to describe what is in the photo, move into remembering other photos or landscapes or wild places or animals or holidays that are evoked from the first few minutes of writing.

Throughout this practice, strive for accuracy. Not literal accuracy. I am not suggesting that every detail of the tree in the photograph gets written in such a way as to precisely replicate the photo via words. I do want you to be as precise as possible with images that arise in your mind's eye, from your heart: memories of other related things, feelings—other trees in other landscapes in places you visited as a child, for example.

The idea is to create a photographic image of your own, by writing about a tangible image in front of you. The image you are creating with words may or may not represent some portion of what is actually shown in the photograph. But the aim is to create something that is absolutely visible to you, with as much sound, flavor, texture, taste, scent, and feeling as you can get into words. Imagine you can offer to a reader a beautiful gift: the present moment of your writing.

Another variation on this exercise is to sit with all of your journaling implements at the ready, and stare at a photograph (the more abstract the better) for thirty to sixty seconds. Then turn over the photograph so that the image is not visible. If you are afraid you will "cheat" (look at the photograph in the middle of the writing), it would be best to slip it underneath something to prevent this from happening. Now poised with pen, you begin to snap the shutter on the camera of your mind and heart. Lay out, word by word, sentence upon sentence, the most minute details about the photograph you studied. If your memory fails (which I hope it does), you are then free to recreate something that may not at all resemble the photograph you chose. Regardless, the mission is to look with the memory of the heart and capture in the phrases you use an image that is as shining, as readable, as knowable as the tree in the photograph. Lion, abstract collage, river in valley, leaking faucet. The subject is irrelevant; the clarity is paramount.

Photographic Clarity:

1. Carefully choose an abstract photograph to use for this writing practice.
    a. The less defined the image, the better.
    b. A strong reaction is a good guide for choosing (love or distaste, enticed or repulsed).
2. If the image is easy to recognize, turn it a quarter or half turn before you begin to write.

3. Spend at least five to ten minutes writing, keeping your pen moving the entire time.

4. Write with as much detail as you can exactly what you see in the photograph.

   a. Describe the shapes you see.

   b. Describe the colors you observe.

   c. Use as much detail as possible.

5. If the words take you to a memory, a feeling, or an experience, explore it in as much detail as you can.

6. Keep writing until the words stop flowing, or until ten minutes are up—whichever comes last.

The Gentler Practice:

1. Choose a photograph of something or someone you are not very familiar with.

2. Spend ten minutes writing down what you see in the photo.

3. Use all five senses in your writing: sight, sound, smell, taste, touch.

4. When the time is up, write one sentence about anything that comes to mind (related to the photo or not).

The Deeper Practice:

1. Follow #s 1-5 in the Photographic Clarity practice.

2. Now, just allow whatever words come next to land on your page.

3. Spend another ten minutes following this stream of writing, being sure to add as much detail as possible.

4. Make your descriptions as accurate and specific as you can.

5. Read what you have written.

6. Add any words that will make what you have written even clearer.

Essay: Body of Water

Our origin as a human individual, remember it or not, began in the swimmingly comfortable ooze of our mother's womb. We all came from there. We received our oxygen in water before we found it in air. We felt the cushion and sway, the warmth and darkness, the easy flow of curled limbs floating in blissful rest. There was little separation between the liquid outside of our skin and that which our growing little forms contained within. Skin, wet and wild, helped to shape and contain legs, arms, head, a protruding nose. We were one with our environment as unborn humans. The outer landscape of amniotic fluid supported us, kept us alive, bedded and blanketed us. It fed us nutrients and breath-in-oxygen-in-water. We trusted the fluid; or if not us consciously, our bodies knew how to receive and respond. Innate wisdom.

I spent my childhood swimming in chlorinated pools and the salty ocean. My mother taught me how to swim when I was four years old. "Reach, cup and grab, pull. Kick. Relax." She was not on the beach when a friend's mother drove me to the ocean many summer mornings and my long, loose hair tangled around my face as the waves of the not-calm Pacific tousled me. Diving under the foam I was free from the turbulence. My sun-scorched child's body acclimated easily to the cooler ocean climate. Many moments were choke-filled saltwater ones, but many others were the peace of floating, body surfing, wading. Or the gaiety of splashing and jumping and diving. When I submerged, my body knew how to hold in my breath and surrender to the water's pressure, different from air.

Water was ever so precious in the hot, perpetually-sunny climate in which I was raised. My family never discussed the fact that we lived so near the desert that, essentially, we were only several inches of annual precipitation away from the designation of "desert." We had a great uncle of Irish descent who lived in the desert proper. The several-hour, sweaty drive to visit him was tinged with emotional upset; my very desert-unfriendly family sacrificed the ease of a slightly greener, cooler home place in order to make our biennial trek. Someone inevitably ended up with heat stroke. We loved this funny, old uncle even though his choice of retirement locales was the burden we bore. We made such a strong demarcation between "his desert" and our comfort.

The sprinkler system that watered our drought-threatened yard seemed a portent: a sign that all was well as long as the appearance of green grass remained. Sometimes the over-watered yard contained very temporary mud patches; puddles lasted about fifteen minutes before the dry air sucked it all into oblivion. But I was a nature-hungry girl (who turned into a nature-dependent woman) and I took advantage of those brief wet moments by using water to write "invisible ink" messages on sidewalks, and mud as an outdoor substitute for Play-Doh. So imagine my embarrassment when, out of laziness, I failed to show up to hand-water the neighbor's lawn during their weeklong summer family vacation. I didn't mind not being paid for the job I agreed to do but, in fact, neglected. But the emotional repercussion of irresponsibility in the face of what we all held dear, a lush grassy yard, was too much. I cried big fat child tears. All pretense of well-being vanished as their grass turned to yellow straw—the very antithesis of everything we'd been taught to value.

After a childhood like that—craving, seeking, overusing, aesthetically dependent upon water—it is no wonder I am an adult who has chosen a very wet, verdant landscape to call "home." I now live in a climate where sunny days are the exception: the polar opposite of my childhood place. I now live in a perpetually-wet, misty, rainy, rainbow-apt locale. I now live on an island in a huge body of saltwater. There is green grass everywhere nearly year-round with no need for sprinklers. Trees are lush and full for three seasons each year, and springtime leaves are as fat as sandwiches. In the winter, we see a deeper green grass and the olive-dark green of fir trees. We do not lack moisture, rarely have droughts. Thick, water-logged mosses cling to any surface available.

I love the curtains of cool humidity that define my chosen home geography. I am one with this landscape.

Ice, snow, rain, dew or frost, ponds, oceans, lakes, rivers, and streams: in every season we receive the bounty of water on the land and we remember how we are, essentially, big bodies of water ourselves. Recall that the human body is about sixty percent water. Our hearts exceed 70% water; no wonder watery tears (indicators of emotion) connect our hearts to the waters of the outer landscape.

Body of Water Practice

Locate an accessible body of water near where you live. In extreme situations where water is not plentiful at the surface, place a pool or large bowl of water on your porch or in your yard. The first part of this practice is to recall a memory from your childhood in which you played in water.

You might recall a visit to the ocean or daily summer swims in the lake; bathtub play or skipping your feet through rain puddles; splashing your hands through a fountain; building a snow person; or the feeling of a light, foggy mist on your upturned cheeks. Remember where you were and how it felt to have the water on your skin or the ice cold snow seeping through your gloves. Try to piece together the memory so that you have enough details to flesh out a movie-like image of the young child you were. What can you remember of the sensation of the water-based substance and the emotions that went along with that? What was fun, enjoyable, frivolous about that experience?

Now you are going to invoke the small child within you in order to have an enjoyable experience of water as an adult. If it is warmer weather as you read this, it will be easier to begin; swimming or wading tends to be more comfortable for people when the air temperature rises. But even in the colder months in your area, you can definitely enjoy this practice. This is intended to be a year-round activity (as are all the practices), so in whichever season you find yourself currently, determine how you can make this practice doable for yourself.

If it is wintertime go skiing or snowshoeing; build something from icicles or snow; make a snow angel, roll in the powder, or walk in the falling snow. If it is summertime, a swim or a legs-dangle into any water body works well for this practice. In the autumn, consider finding a different water body—perhaps a mud hole from the onset of rain, or dance under the dripping wet boughs of a tree limb you have just shaken down upon yourself. Even better, go outside during a rainstorm and allow yourself to get soaking wet; no umbrella is necessary, perhaps not even a raincoat. (Dare I say that going naked outside in the rain in a private place can be very liberating?) During the vernal season you might choose to find a new spring, or go to a place where the river runs high from snowmelt; immerse—for however long you can tolerate—your fingers or toes, or wash your face in the ice cold water.

The most important part of this practice is to become immersed emotionally, as well as to whatever degree you can immerse in the water physically. Push an edge or boundary; abandon responsibility for few minutes. If the winter's or spring's water play causes you to shriek in delight or shock from the cold, you have accomplished the practice. If the water experience in warmer months reminds you of an earlier time in your life, or refreshes you, it is a well-done practice. If you choose to totally immerse yourself in the water body, see if you can swim in imitation of a beaver, otter, seabird, Olympian, or float like a fallen leaf on the surface. Flail your arms; swing your feet; hold your breath as you douse your head; move backwards or upside down; do a handstand at depth; flow with the water.

Feel what it is like to be a bag of water *in* water. How can you feel the water from the outside seeping inward and the moisture within you merging with that of the outside water body? How can you imagine the saltwater of your tears merging with the salinity of the bay? What within you is moss-covered and a bit moldy, or pungent like seaweed? How is your inner water as clear as the dewdrops or sparkly as ice? Where do your inner waters overflow and into what do they spill? What edges or berms keep your internal waters reined in? Most germane, how does it feel to move your body in the almost-weightless environment of the water—even if it is only your hands in an icy winter stream or a bowl on your porch?

As you engage your writing project ask the water, "How can you help me flow?" Then put your hands or feet in water and experience the flow of liquid around them. Go back to your manuscript with open-ended inquiry as your mindset. Let your typing fingers take charge of the content.

Body of Water:

1. Locate a body of water near you.
2. Recall a childhood memory involving water play.
3. Flesh out the memory with details.
4. Swim, ski, splash, roll, wade, dip in the water source; at the very least let your hands play in the water, or let the water drip on you.
5. Explore how (part of) your body feels moving in the watery environment.

The Gentler Practice:

1. Fill a bowl, or your tub, with a little bit of warm water.
2. Place your hands, or feet, in the water.
3. Close your eyes and feel the water on your body.
4. Remember a time when you enjoyed water as a little child.

The Deeper Practice:

1. Follow #s 1-5 in the Body of Water practice.
2. Do this until you can find the pure joy in it.
3. Feel what it is like to be a bag of water *in* water.
4. Take the feeling of the flow of water back to your writing.

Chapter Five

OUR MIND AND THE LANDSCAPE OF MOUNTAINTOP AIR

This chapter explores our intellect in relationship to writing, especially as we breathe life into the structure of our writing. The practices here include: charting the patterns in our writing process, making choices about tasks involved with our projects, and following curiosity about nature to better understand our personal process of seeking knowledge about the content of our writing.

Mountaintop Air

Our minds can serve our writing very well, in balance with all other parts of ourselves (body, emotion, spirit). We seek the heights of a mountain ridge for the panoramic view of the landscape; so, too, we are able to find perspective, information, and insight as we climb the trail to greater knowledge. Climbing the mountain trail we find switchbacks, sharp or gentle. After a short while, we begin to feel we know the pattern of that trail—whether it is wide or narrow, steep or grandly sloping, tightly curved or meandering. We see the patterns in our writing process and what it takes to reach a written outcome that we need or want, and this is good information for us. Sometimes we take a hiking path and suddenly come to a fork; after considering for a moment, we simply proceed. There is always something to learn—or from which we can grow ourselves, our project—by taking whichever path we choose.

So, too, there is always something we can do to serve our writing, even in the moments when we are not putting words on the page. Research, reading, finding what we need, editing: these are tasks we may well need to do for our writing project. They serve the outcome. As we trod over the dirt or pebbles, sand or moss, to the clear air of the mountain's ridgetop, we discover something that catches our attention. We explore that thing, asking questions or seeking information about it. This is also what we do in writing, especially as we expand our repertoire of written material to include forgotten memories or facts, as we seek others' expert knowledge about a topic, or as we strive to add detail to our writing; we get curious and follow our noses to something new.

Like standing in the breeze at the apex of our climb, we breathe in heavily the scent of wind-cleansed, nature-scented air. We see broadly and with clarity, above the particulate matter of lower elevations.

Our Mind's Relationship to Writing

Most of us easily recognize how important our cognitive functions are to writing; in common parlance, "It's a no-brainer." Imagine, though, that intellect includes the thought processes associated with survival; the frigid season of winter offers us good examples. We are clever, and imbued with innate survival skills. Many of us turn to books, journaling, and quiet indoor tasks during the wintertime, to retreat from the chill. Our bodies are not impervious to the cold. We have looked at how our bodies and our emotions are integral to writing. Now, we explore how our brains come to the fore, how they get to do the work they long to do in the writing endeavor. Intellect and thought, planning ahead, and being ready for the possibilities (of writing) are also features of wintertime: the hasty or ill-prepared get caught in harsh conditions; but those who have created a structure that supports long dark chilly nights simply endure in well-being. Rationality, order, boundaries, cognition serve us well as we navigate the outer landscapes in winter; they also serve us well as we greet the frigid difficulty of writing.

The mind is thought and applied skill, but it is equally the ability to endure. When our bodies or emotions are weak, we can sometimes garner the strength we need to keep on going by thoughtfully remembering we have been here before and will move through this harder landscape once again. We use our good brains to remember that we do know how to survive—the harshness of literal natural seasons as well as the hard seasons of our writing.

Essay: Logging the Journey

Years ago as part of my undergraduate degree, I enrolled in a natural history course that included several field study camping trips. The ecology-based class required that we devise, design, and engage in nature-based research during the final weekend trip. With a novice's interest in qualitative research (methodologies I extensively studied, used, and honed later in graduate school) and with abiding passions for both the natural world as well as creativity, I decided to explore the impact of differing biomes on my writing. It just so happened that we were camped in a place that included several different natural areas coming together in this particular wilderness location; it offered a stark contrast of settings in which to conduct my project. I chose the sage scrub desert area and the riparian zone as my two test areas. My research involved looking at how I responded to writing as I sat for half a day in each of these natural areas.

For the first part of the day I sat in a low camping chair in the middle of an open patch of land. There were low sage bushes all around me and it was a very arid area. The sun was scorching that late spring day, and I had with me a notebook and pens. I journaled as I sat there for hours, remembering things from my childhood and everything I had been taught about the desert. I got a terrible headache by the end of my time there. The next part of my study took place under the shade of beautiful willow trees lining a rushing river. I felt cool and soothed by the area. I ended up lying down in the grass along the bank and falling into a deep sleep. I barely wrote anything while I was there, in contrast to the pages and pages I had written during my desert time. One of the crucial things I learned about my own creativity in relationship to natural environments is that I need a mix of comfort and edginess in order to be productive in my creative pursuits. I was overly uncomfortable in the desert area, and overly soothed on the river's edge. While I produced a lot of written material in the sage scrub area, it was not of a very high quality; I also made myself sick by not doing proper self-care when my body got overheated. One of my conclusions was that my creativity depends on the *inspiration* from beautiful and comfortable natural areas, but that my best writing could not effectively take place there.

Finding this balance of what aids or hinders us as we engage the challenging task of writing is a significant step toward honing our writing practice. Though it seems so obvious in retrospect, I'm not sure I would have ever learned—without this experience—that my writing is not best conducted at the river's edge. The research process of recording location, place, time, weather conditions, writing process, written outcome, and the other details as I engaged the project gave me a tangible accounting of what *really* happened out there. No matter what I preferred to believe going into that study (first hypothesis: the comfortable area will spur me to write great quantities and lovely content), the log I had kept showed me the *actual* results.

Discovering the edge where we are not too cozy (I urge aspiring writers *not* to take their computers to bed with them) and not too uncomfortable can push us further in our writing. So a writer needs a record, an accounting of where she has been on her journey. Just like a travel diary, a writing log can yield important information about how our writing is going: where we have been, what we are doing when we are there, how it felt, of what it consisted, and when it was we journeyed through our writing tasks. Very importantly, this is not a tool for criticizing oneself. It is especially designed to see what works for our writing and what factors contribute to a feeling of well-being and productivity.

The writer who keeps a log of his writing progress begins to see patterns: the frequency with which he visits his written work, how he feels at the end of the writing session, and what he wrote about. These are all really helpful tools for productivity in writing. One of the most important pieces of the writing log is the time of day that the writing happens. But this bit of information is not enough. Each aspect of the writing log is in relationship to the others; the result is that the writer can get a really good snapshot of his writing experience from day to day. From this he can see what does work and what does not really work very well toward productivity and satisfaction with his writing.

Reviewing a writing log, the writer learns something about her process—the day of the week, and the time that she has spent working on her book, essay, paper, chapter, poetry, or memoir. She realizes that there are differences between the length of time she spends writing in the morning, for example, and how long she has spent writing at the end of the day. The length of time can be a crucial indicator about preferred writing style. If she notices that every time she writes in the evening, she is only spending a few minutes, but her morning writing sessions extend for two hours, then she can carve out more time earlier in the day to get going on writing. However, if she is more satisfied with the writing she does in shorter stints, this is valuable information about the *quality* of the final product.

We cannot always greatly alter our writing time, especially if we have other responsibilities that add constraints and demands to our schedule. But we can capitalize on what works for us, and aim toward that—little by little. One writer might notice that she is able to draft more pages on the weekend, specifically on Saturday afternoon. She begins to tell people she is busy on Saturday afternoons but can get together in the morning that day. Writing often takes a back seat to the other things in a person's life; this is because writing is perceived as hard. And sometimes it really *is* difficult, or part of what we are writing is difficult. Writing takes concentration and skill. If we are unable to give attention and nurturance to ourselves, we will have a hard time figuring out how to give them to others, or to our writing.

A writing log is a tool to give the new or aspiring writer a sense of his patterns. By reviewing the log, writers see at a glance what has or has not been working in their writing schedule. And from all of this, the writer gleans the conditions that make her writing ripe! With this information in mind, the writer can make adjustments and maximize his own best writing by moving toward consistency within his unique landscape of writing.

Writing Log Practice

On a landscape-oriented sheet of paper in a journal, add the title "Writing Log." Make the following seven column headings: date, time of day, length of time, amount, content, feeling, and location. In the first column include the date (month and day number) and the day of the week. The time of day needs to be very specifically marked as AM or PM following the start time for that particular writing session. For length of time, there should be a good guess of how long you have actually spent putting words down on the page. Sometimes writers stare at the screen (or page) for a while before and during a writing session. If these non-typing moments are actual thinking and composing time, then they count as "writing." If you are doing research, checking email, sending text messages back and forth, daydreaming about a wonderful social activity from the night before, you are probably not doing much in service to the composition; this would not count as length of time spent writing, even if the computer is on and the document is open in front of you.

The amount of writing that you log into your journal is usually represented by the number of pages you have written during that session. If you are working on an extensive document (such as a research paper, thesis, dissertation, book), you might be adding paragraphs to different sections of the document in a single writing session. The easiest way to keep track of these is to note the number of pages already in the document at the onset of the session and then the number at the end. Both of these numbers can go in the "amount" column. (You can also look at the word count at the beginning and end in order to chart the amount of progress.) Remember that any writing (words being added to the page) counts as the amount. So if you are outlining, brainstorming on the page, drafting paragraphs, taking notes that will be expanded into sentences, these count as "writing." Words on a page. The closer the notes and words on a page resemble the voice, tone, and semantics you intend to use in the paper, the better; these translate more readily into sentences than do abbreviations or shorthand notes. (For example, if what you are composing uses the same technical or specific phrasing repeatedly, it is simpler in the long run to write these out each time in the notes so that when you begin the hard-core drafting, you don't have to go back and type in the full term.)

Content is the next column in the writing log. It is best if the short phrase or sentence that you note into the log is as specific as possible. For academic papers requiring citations and references, for example, having spent the entire writing session working on the bibliographic information is crucial to note in your log. While the source information is vital and necessary to academic or scholarly work, it requires a different type of focus and concentration than the drafting of the paper. You will have a much better sense of your writing patterns (and thus your writing *needs*) if you are able to glance at the log and see *when* you wrote *what* for this project. If you're working on a memoir or essay, for example, note which section you worked on that particular day and at that specific time.

Noting, too, how the writing session *felt* is a very valuable tool for somebody who needs to write extensively for academic, professional, or personal purposes. Perhaps you composed five pages but feel they are not your best work, that they were a struggle and will need more extensive editing and redrafting later. Or, you may have experienced an easy flow to that section of the writing project, enjoying the task of composition that you endeavored in that day. Finding a word or short phrase that very clearly sums up your feeling at the end of the session is instructive; over time you will see which aspects of the writing are more challenging for you, and which are easier. You will notice that which is interesting or those parts of the project that bore you. Sometimes free-flowing writing emerges when we feel less constrained by structure; other times a writer will need guidelines set forth for the project that are either imposed by some authority—professor, publisher, genre form—or set by the writer himself. Noting whether your writing is facilitated or hindered by such structures will lend valuable information about your writing style and process; these can help you better formulate plans for the next writing project— plans that capitalize on your strengths and that provide work-arounds for your writing challenges.

Finally, noting location is key: where you were actually situated during that writing session. The living room couch, at a desk in your private study, in a public place (be specific), at the kitchen table, at a friend's house, in an airport. Some people choose the same spot for writing each time. Others like and need to roam around a bit. Just noting where it was that the writing took place can be helpful, even if the writing is always in the same spot. For example, if you are continually impeded in your writing (seeing from the log that sessions are not very productive or satisfying) but you continue to sit at the desk in your office, you may want to move the next writing session to a different location. Try things. See what works. And go where the (writing) flow is!

The setting in which you choose to write includes not only the location but also the environment around you as you write. Though you don't need to add this category to your writing log—simpler is preferable—please do pay attention to your surroundings. Noise, lighting, interruptions, seating arrangement, and others' activity can all contribute to how you make (or do not make) progress during a writing session. In the university town I lived in during the early writing of this book, I noticed many students utilizing Starbuck's free Wi-Fi as they sat with laptops open. Some used ear buds, others chatted with people at neighboring tables, and still others looked as if they would bore a hole into their screens with the sheer concentration they exhibited. Even at home we have neighbors (especially for people living in multiple unit dwellings), people outside with noisy lawn equipment, family members, roommates, children or pets; in short, other people living in or around us make noise and go about their lives—whether we have something to write or not. Just pay attention to these things as you review your writing log each day, and then on a weekly basis. If you started out not really knowing which writing conditions work well for you, or what patterns of showing up to the page you tend to exhibit, take comfort in the writing log. It is a tool to help you see your patterns.

Writing Log:

1. Title your landscape-oriented sheet, "Writing Log."
2. Make seven columns.
3. Label each column with one of the following: date, time of day, length of time, amount, content, feeling, and location.
4. Complete all seven columns for each writing session.
5. After one month, look back at the writing log and notice when you felt good about your writing session.

The Gentler Practice:

1. Follow #1 in the Writing Log practice.
2. Make three columns with the following labels: date, time of day, feeling.
3. Complete each column for every writing session.
4. After one week, look at the writing log and see when you felt good about your writing session.

The Deeper Practice:

1. Follow #s 1-4 in the Writing Log practice.
2. After one week, look at your writing log to find the patterns in your writing.
   a. What time of day do you tend to spend the most time writing?
   b. What is the average amount of time for each writing session?
   c. When do you leave your writing feeling the most pleased?
   d. How many pages did you write this week?
3. Model this week's writing after the best of last week's—choose the time of day that left you feeling the most productive or pleased.
4. Week after week continue to keep the writing log and look for patterns that work for you and your writing.

Essay: Always Something

There are people (mostly those who do not write at all) who believe writing is frivolous; that it is simple, unnecessary, boring (to write or read); or that it is an exclusive and singular task. It is not; especially the latter: it is not just the act of putting fingers on keyboard and typing away. Composing a written piece is a very complex and multifarious activity that can involve many related tasks. Getting into the writing, navigating through the draft, polishing the work, and completing the project involve many steps and necessitate the willingness to go through various stages with the writing. Here, I offer a number of practices that can foster the first item in the list above: getting into the landscape of the writing. This is really difficult for many of us. Sometimes it does feel like jumping into the icy cold river and being carried downstream a bit.

The trees are thick, providing deep shade along the banks of the river. Because it is springtime (literally right now as I type this), the water is more a fast, frigid highway of leaf litter, twigs, and unsuspecting insects than it is a meandering respite for hot summer days. Blackbirds sit along the flanks, in bushes overhanging the water, and then suddenly lift into flight to grab another perch. Songbirds hidden high in the thick leaves of alders sing their hearts out in harmonies too numerous to pick out, and the woodpecker rattles his own head along the trunk of the storm-ridden snag. Everything is loud, moving, crashing, rushing. Yet it is also perfectly inviting. Without a second thought a human finger reaches down, an arm stretches, a knee bends, and the sting of the cold catches the swimmer in a gasp of shock, fear, and delight. This is an intrepid water crawler, one who knows that the invigoration of being in the river is worth every second of the skin-numbing cold that will be the first immersion. The only question in her mind is whether to undergo the adjustment to the cold slowly, or to suddenly jump in—whole body stunned and focused into that first sudden scream of pain and thrill.

Like the swimmer, the writer makes a choice each and every time she sits down to write. She either jumps in with her whole body—feeling the sharp, cold white of the snowy blank page to tell the guts of whatever her story is in that moment ... or ... she takes one toe and dips it in slowly, letting her skin adjust to the temperature of the writing for that day. Movement—slowly like an acclimation, or quickly like the rush of the fast-submerged technique—will vary for the writer from writing session, to project, to time, to life circumstances.

Sometimes though, the choice is not clear. The way through to the writing is crowded and clogged; the computer is buried underneath the rubble of the inner landscape. In this situation, there are ways to further the writing that do not necessarily involve actual typing into a document. Other sections of this book have discussed free-writes and journaling. I refer the writer who cannot seem to make fingers animate letters into words that form a story onto the page right back to these practices. Often the free-writes can get us unstuck. The journaling offers a refuge from structure, format, and content. In both journaling and free-writing, we release ourselves from anything other than what is really going on within us (even if what is going on within us is directly linked to what is going on around us). In short, these practices bring us back to the immediacy and emotion of this precise second. No more. No less. It is very empowering, too.

One morning I was working with a client who had made a commitment to engage her writing a specific number of times each week. Her project was fresh and new; it was exciting to her. She was working on a story—*her* story—that had grown over decades, become wiser with time and experience, deepened and become rich. A decadent, complex, savory stew of a story this woman had. However, despite carrying her writing materials with her as she went on a small road trip, she did not write even once: not one sentence. (Her email to me upon return had a subject line that read, "Not one word.") What happened to her as she did a free-write with me during our session changed her. In a timed, five-minute, prompt-less free-write, this woman discovered what had been holding her back from writing that week. The very thing she adored—her story—had gotten sullied by an interaction with a loved on: the very beloved who is central to my client's story. There had been some emotionally uncomfortable exchange between them. My client had divulged some things about her story; her loved one's response did not serve the woman's story and, additionally, was deeply painful to her.

However, the free-write during our session that morning ended up doing just that: freeing the writer. In a few short minutes of writing in her journal, the client realized that the combination of painful emotions and the story itself had become fused; the woman turned her angst and sadness around the challenging emotional experience into distaste for her own story. Once she became clear about this, my client found her way back into motivation to engage her story, her writing.

Jumping, or easing our way, into the icy pool of our writing can be accomplished sometimes a bit indirectly.

Always Something To Do Practice

If the following are done with an intention for moving forward with the writing, they can be fully trustworthy to do so. An intention can be as short as: *While I do this, I will hold the idea of my writing.* Or, *This thing I'm about to do is in service to my writing.* Or, *I will act as if doing this thing will actually push me into my writing and story.*

Hand Writing. If you are stuck—especially in this electronics-dominated world of cell phones (and text messages), computers, and Word documents—please consider cultivating a relationship again with writing by hand. (We learned to write this way.) You can do this through free-writes and journaling. The client who quickly realized what had kept her from working on her story also realized how to untangle herself so that she could move through and back to her writing; so can you.

There are plenty of other ways to use handwritten notes and memos to move forward with your writing project. For example, a handwritten card can help move you. One or two sentences tucked inside a card—sent off to a friend or loved one—can be just the small yet tangible step back toward your center, your core, the place from which writing comes.

Transcribe Handwriting. Another task that can be in service to our actual typewritten story is to transcribe what we have handwritten, including notes about the story, into our computer. I often have ideas or insights (or even something I am quite sure I will need to reject as unnecessary to the story); I scribble these on scraps of paper that I keep in a small basket on my desk. If I am feeling especially "dry" as I sit down at the computer—that is, I am sure that I do not have anything to say that is good, useful, that moves and furthers the story I am working on (e.g., book, scholarly article, informal blog post)—I take these scraps of notes and ill-formed ideas, and type them into the computer. I actually have a document for this very book I am writing. It is called "Notes." This document is my catch-all for things I am thinking about and want to remember in regard to this book. I keep adding descriptions of various landscapes and landscape features in this document, synonyms for words I am using frequently here, alternative subtitles for the book, practices I want to include, and structural formatting ideas. Sometimes, too, when I have just had a long writing session on the book and then move into another activity (especially one that involves moving my body through space), when I have discussed the book with a loved one, or when I've read a section to one of my writing partners, I will suddenly be struck with another idea. I scribble these down, saving them for the next writing session.

Sometimes, according to what I am sure is some universal law of writing, I can count on ideas coming to me when I am not in a position to write them down. Some of my greatest moments of writing inspiration (the actual desire to sit down *right now* and type into my book) come when I am: out in the wilderness with no shelter, electricity, or computer; walking the dog on the beach; taking a shower; sitting down to a special meal with friends; or up against a deadline on a project totally unrelated to my book. I realized, after nearly two years of having a particular type of cell phone, that I can make voice memos whenever I unexpectedly have a writing idea. When I'm in the wilderness now, I always have a journal and pens with me. Later, I transcribe these into a computer document. I have found that this has been an invaluable aid to my memory when I really do put aside all distractions (real or perceived) and sit down to compose another section of another chapter of my book.

Organize Files. Also greatly in service to our writing is file organization. I have helped many clients create electronic organization systems for their big writing projects. We start with one very easily recognizable file folder in the electronic documents file list; we name it something short and simple. We then open that electronic folder and create blank documents formatted for the project; we include a header (including the writer's name and the page number), and a title ("Chapter A" is fine if you're not ready to commit to a particular topic or name for what you are writing about). I have also had clients who have made it many pages and chapters into their writing project but have absolutely no organizing principle whatsoever. The computer files are disorganized. Sorting these out is time-consuming at best. In the worst case, I had a client who hired me just after "losing" some important sections of her big writing project. It turns out they were not lost as much as "hidden"— tucked away in some obscure electronic file with an unrelated label. We sorted it all out and placed the missing sections back into their proper place.

This is also the case with written files. Some writers use archives of notes, letters, photographs, old drafts, research, and correspondence to help in writing their complex work. Taking some time to organize these into labeled cardstock file folders—simply touching and looking at photos or old journals—can move us toward the keyboard once again.

No matter how you choose to organize, or how much you dislike the word or notion of "organizing," it will be of invaluable support to you as you climb through the brambles of a complicated or multilayered writing project. This is so important—and so foreign to many creatives whose forte is in letting the inspiration lead while the structures take a rest—that I have led workshops, courses, presented about, and mentored weeks of client time through very simple (and painless, some admit later) procedures for handling difficult projects. The key is to keep the system as simple and consistent as possible.

Walk in Nature. I can recall countless stories about how being out in the natural world has inspired, clarified, solved, relieved any number of passages in any number of writing projects I have ever done. I have already written about some of them in this book. Indeed, this is the whole point of this book: the pairing of nature and writing toward wholeness. So all I need to say here is this: nature helps us. If you feel stuck or have a problem, need a break, experience boredom about your written work or project, go outside. But do not go out forever, abandoning the writing altogether. Do go out with the thoughts, issues, or ennui rolling around inside you. Look around. Move a little. And, go back in to the writing page refreshed.

Read Through Writing. Sometimes I am closer to being able to add words to my manuscript than I *feel* like I am. If my resistance or fuzzy-headedness feels less than on the really-big-writing-block or I'm-so-stuck-I-can't-imagine-how-I'll-get-words-onto-the-page days, then I know that just a little nudge will help. The small movement I take is to read something I've written right before I put my hands on a pen or the keyboard. I might read one paragraph or one page, but I read my own written words. Of course, I try to choose a section of the writing that is pleasing to me— where the miracle of an unexpectedly beautiful word or phrase arrived on the page without my forethought, a section that is especially interesting or reminds me of something I like or enjoy, a snippet that rings so true that changing a single letter would make it dishonest. You don't need to spend a long time searching for the right passage, or find yourself totally in love with a section you've written. In a desperate moment, just read the very last sentence you wrote.

Doing this read-before-writing activity aids us in several ways. First, it reminds us where we left off in the writing: remembering what content we have already covered and seeing what we need to add, how we need to clarify. It also helps us get back in the style of the particular written piece: the language choices, the tense, the feeling tone. Also, reading what we have written just before writing the next bit reminds us of the purpose of the piece: who the audience is, what the goal is for the writing, the reason we are endeavoring to write this thing in the first place.

All the while you must be sure to hold the intention of moving forward in your writing by doing these tasks. Because the temptation to use any of these activities as a diversion can be as alluring as a cool evening breeze after a sweltering heat wave. "Procrastination," that despicable word to some aspiring writers, is an act of *moving away from* the writing; a two-week long activity of sorting out childhood photos at the expense of your writing session exemplifies what I mean by this. Remember: you want the "something" you are doing to move you *toward* the writing.

The real trick with these strategies is that sometimes they can push a writer right into the depths of her book, research paper, or memoir without even being aware that it is happening. All of a sudden she realizes she has traveled down the river to the next large boulder and is sunning her body atop the rock with a great feeling of accomplishment.

Now choose from the list above and *go!*

Always Something To Do:

1. Set a timer for thirty minutes for any of the following activities.
    a. With your writing project in mind, try handwriting in your journal or on a blank sheet of paper. Or handwrite a greeting card to a loved one. Take notes about your story or writing project.
    b. Transcribe notes, project ideas, and other handwritten material onto the typed computer page.
    c. With your writing project in mind, organize your paper files and notes for the writing project. Or, organize your computer files.
    d. With your writing project in mind, take a short walk in nature.
    e. Read through what you have already written—on the computer screen, in the notebook, or as a printed out (paper) copy.
2. Choose one item from the list (a-e) and do it for the duration of your set time.
3. But then, return. Return to the writing page. Write.
4. Type as fast as you can into the document knowing that later you can add, delete, or edit anything that doesn't serve you or the needs of the project.

The Gentler Practice:

1. Set a timer for five minutes.
2. For that entire time, scribble notes or questions about your writing project onto a piece of paper.
3. When it goes off, reset the timer for another five minutes.
4. Gather all of your books, notes and questions, and resources for the writing project; put them near your writing spot.
5. Set the timer one last time, for five minutes.
6. Looking at the books, notes, papers for your writing project, identify the very next small thing you know how to do to continue the writing. This might be a word, phrase, outside source/reference, Idea, or a heading you can add.
7. Open your document and type in that very next small thing.

The Deeper Practice:

1. Follow #s 1-2 in the Always Something To Do practice.
2. Think about the most difficult dilemma in your writing project.
3. Imagine that you possess or can easily obtain everything you need to work through this problem.
4. Make a list of what you need.
5. Identify what you already have on your needs list, as well as what you will need to do to obtain the rest.
6. Gather one thing you already have.
7. Commit to getting—within the next twenty-four hours—one thing you need that you don't already have.
8. Open your document, typing as fast as you can into it. Later you can add, delete, or edit anything that doesn't serve you or the needs of the project.

Essay: Identification of Nature

Getting to know something requires attention, and we can easily begin to know something or someone by following our interests during those moments of attentiveness. As we begin to write our paper, book, story—even our résumé—we are confronted with the need to convey particular pieces of information. Sometimes we know what that information is; other times we need to apply our minds in service to learning or gathering the needed information.

During graduate school, I was assigned a final course research project applying various ecological tools and methodologies that had been part of that semester's curriculum. Because I had developed such a strong connection to the land on which I was newly residing, I opted to conduct my research right there on the property—three thousand miles across the country from the deeply familiar terrain in which I'd spent most of my life. I would look at the edge where the field met the forest.

*   *   *

I lived in a rustic apartment on the top floor of what had been, for decades, the barn on the working farm. Hand-hewn beams and an A-frame ceiling were just a few of the reminders of the apartment's former purpose. A wide wooden balcony overlooked the front field, and just beyond that stood a dense, mature forest of birch trees. In the far distance was a lake backed by a short ridge of hills.

One hundred acres of wooded, thick, rugged land on which to live, to roam throughout four distinct seasons. To explore and learn about at will. All at a bargain price, and during the years when my need for outdoor respite was punctuated by twelve to fifteen hours a day with my head buried in books and focused on computer screens, deep in environmental research and study. I lightheartedly joked with my graduate cohort buddies about the irony of being in an ecology-based program that required so much book and computer work (primarily done indoors, of course).

I took at least an hour every morning at first light to sip coffee, with field guides and binoculars next to me. As dawn rose, I would observe the movements and flashes of color of the bird life. Goldfinches and bluebirds. Rose-breasted grosbeaks. Cardinals, nuthatches, scarlet tanagers. Bobolinks and brown-headed cowbirds, in addition to house wrens and towhees. Even wild turkeys. I had heard a few of these bird names, but I had never seen or really *known* them before living on the east coast. Others were brand new avian explorations for me. I usually started the identification process by paying attention to a flash of color—a red glint in sunlight, or deep blue against tree bark. I was also very drawn in by the shapes of bills and the textures of feathers. Sometimes it was their behavior that caught my attention: the way a wild turkey walked in a straight line behind a tree trunk, blocking my line of sight as he hurriedly walked away. Or the nuthatch's upside down foraging on that same trunk. And, very unfortunately, I had my first experience of regular bird strikes; the sliding glass door to my deck, though very dirty, was a target for a number of birds who hit hard, fell, and did not always recover. I developed a ritual for burying the birds who died from such strikes. For the first time in my life, I maintained a number of different types of bird feeders on that splintery old deck overhanging the field. Suet, sunflower seeds, millet, corn, sugar water. I also learned which scampering animals liked to drain the feeders before birds had a chance to sate themselves.

As the seasons transitioned in that new and temporary landscape, I felt the subtle changes in weather. I noticed which creatures visited the property, inhaled the scents of trees or wet soil, carefully gathered edible mushrooms for dinner. Each season I would find ways to be outside, teaching myself things I'd always dreamed of doing: cross-country skiing in winter, picking ripe fruit off the vine in summer, learning the names of birds by the quiet early light of a spring morning, taking brisk forest walks under the fiery autumn canopy. These were very full days, seasons, a total of several years. I adored that apartment, the gatherings I hosted for my cohort (fellow humans), and the visitations of so many intriguing nonhumans.

*   *   *

I conducted that graduate course research project on the transition zone between the field and the forest where I lived; these rich areas of biological convergence are referred to as "ecotones." I have long had a passion for what resides at the edges: two biomes coming together, the interplay of oil and water on a canvas, collages of items found in nature, life transitions, birth and death, grief and love. So an ecological study that used scientific principles to examine that parcel of land that was not-totally-forest-but-not-totally-field excited me. It propelled me. I have always been much more interested in the messy terrain of qualitative research and experience than the oft-thought more tidy realms of numbers and hard science; this project allowed me to indulge in both, and represented an ecotone in and of itself: the merging of the quantification of a place with the aesthetic and qualitative values of that place.

This story illustrates how one moment—one feather, one color, one tree, a field grown tall with grasses in spring but mowed to short hay by late summer—led to a whole exploration of a place. It shows that by following one tiny area of interest or simply noting what captures our attention, we can actually learn something—gain knowledge—in the most organic, natural way. We can move into the collection of information—the data-gathering that will be required of us as we write—if we allow ourselves to be guided by what we *want* to know, doing so bit by bit and deeper into the world of natural curiosity. Little did I know when I sat quietly with my morning coffee and binoculars trained to the tree that I would enter a whole new world of feathered avian delights. Even less, did I expect to learn about squirrels, mice, chipmunks—the visitors to the bird feeders. Nor could I have imagined that one quietly lying fallen bird would suddenly rise up into the sky on wings unmarred by the window's impact, or that the ones who did die and who I buried would lead me to a deeper insight into hospice work and nature-based ceremony. I certainly, in hundreds of days, never would have guessed that my simple year-end study of the ecotone in my backyard would become the metaphor for decades of experience looking at the intersection of inner landscape and outer landscape, or that I would actually be writing this book about it fifteen years later. Following our small curiosities deeper into the world of things—and better—into the rich world of nature and earth, can open up all types of doors and windows into knowledge, insight, information, and wisdom for our lives and for our writing.

Identification of Nature Practice

There is a wealth of information—a body of knowledge—that the earth and its beings innately carry. The wisdom is sometimes in nature's patterns, themes, cycles, and aesthetics. It is also translated into the language of ecology by humans who seek to more deeply know the mechanics and science of the nonhuman living world. There is a way in which we can engage our everyday living world through small bits of knowledge that grow our familiarity, and— perhaps, then—reduce our fear about that which we perceive as so different from us. One simple thing we can do to begin to increase our knowledge about the natural world is to learn the names ascribed to the various plants, animals, insects, and blooming parts. We can start with a name. Then we move to a function or a cycle. We nurture this relationship through observation, touch, and appreciation.

Here is the practice in its barest, initial form. Go to an outdoor space with which you are frequently in contact. Your yard is fine, or a local park, a tree at the edge of a road, your neighbor's bush (with permission, of course). Spend a few minutes noticing what is around you. Pay attention to what you have noticed over and over again as you come into proximity of this living being. If it's the roots of a tree that rise up in wavy patterns at the surface of the soil, stay with that. If it is the one-footed bird—otherwise nondescript—that comes hopping around your cement patio in the cool sunshine, wait in stillness for its arrival again. If something flies, crawls, walks, scurries, saunters, dances, swims, whispers, dances or stands in complete immobility, remain focused on its pathway or presence.

Hold your gaze lightly and your mind freely. Allow something to just "strike" you as interesting, uncommon, prevalent, colorful, active, odd. Consider what you appreciate about this being, or about some particular aspect of it. Think about what confuses or compels you about it. Allow yourself to ask the questions you might have heard your childhood self or another child ask: *Where does that bird go when it is not in my or my neighbor's yard? Where is his nest? How can he keep dry enough in the rain? Of what are his feathers made?* Give yourself a break; allow the questions to be simple. Decide which one or two things you really want to know now that you have spent time exploring these queries in your mind.

Once you have returned home (or at a local library), open a book: dictionary, field guide, encyclopedia. Learn something, however small, about that thing or being in nature that you noticed and had questions about. Pay attention to how you unravel other pieces of information that interest you as you begin to learn about this particular entity. Did you go to a field (nature) guide to look up that bird you saw in the backyard? Was it an online search engine that began to feed you more information about the nesting habits of that finch in the eaves on the front of your house? Note the information and the source. Just for your own edification.

Identification of Nature:

1. Go into an outdoor space with which you are familiar, or to which you often go or pass through.
2. Spend a few minutes just noticing what is around you.
3. Now pay attention to something you see every time you're in this space.
4. Hold your gaze lightly and see what really captures your attention.
5. Consider what captivates or interests you about this creature or feature of this place.
6. Consider what you want to know about it; if it helps you, ask the types of questions children do.
7. Decide what you really want to know *now* about this thing.
8. Go home (or to a library) and seek out the answer.
9. Allow your search for answers to lead you anywhere, to generate new questions, to find closed doors (where no answers seem available).

The Gentler Practice:

1. Go into your yard or a nearby park.
2. Choose one tree or flower that interests you.
3. Come up with one question you would like to know about it.
4. Seek out the answer to your question.
   a. Ask your question to somebody else who might know the answer.
   b. Use a field guide to identify the answer.
   c. Open a (hard copy!) dictionary, encyclopedia, or go to a library to find the answer.
   d. Call a local nature center, parks department, or conservation organization and ask them your question.

The Deeper Practice:

1. Get a sketchbook or notebook and a pen to take with you.
2. Follow #s 1-2 in the Identification of Nature practice.

3. Find something new that you have never noticed before in this space.
4. Name (or identify) this thing, writing it down. If you don't know what it is called, that's okay.
5. Write down everything you can think of about how this thing looks.
6. Draw the plant or creature or object. A scribble or geometric shapes are fine.
7. Write down as many questions as you can think of about it.
8. Decide what two things you want to know about this nature item. If you don't know its name that is the first of the two things you will write down.
9. Go home (or to a library) and seek out the answer.
10. Allow your search for answers to lead you anywhere, to generate new questions, to find closed doors (where no answers seem available).

Chapter Six

OUR SPIRIT AND THE LANDSCAPE OF DESERT SUN

This chapter explores our spirit in relationship to writing, especially demonstrating the crucial role that the fire of our passions plays in our writing life and its outcomes. The practices here include: acknowledging faith's role in our writing as we seek broader insights, creating beauty in the natural world, and nurturing our love for the writing process as well as our specific projects.

Desert Sun

The desert—whether the sandy Sahara or the rocky Death Valley—is a place of stark and shining beauty. It is not without challenge though. The sun, fireball in the sky, is pervasive, hot, glaring. It is the thing that keeps us warm and alive. And without due attention, it can sear us before we know it. Being in a desert requires attentiveness to all parts of ourselves: body, emotion, and mind. We use the strength of our body to endure it. We feel the emotions that it invokes (as it surely will!). We rely on knowledge about how to survive so that we do not succumb to its intensity. But these are all underscored by faith—trust that we will be okay.

As we move deeper into the sometimes stark-naked, unabashed vastness of a desert—oftentimes so foreign to our cluttered landscape of human-built or natural-featured daily life—our vision shifts. We become able to see the broader landscape: those unseeable forces that shape the desert, and which shape our writing. We come to love that energy, force, god, goddess, cactus, or rock that shows up in just the right moment to offer us strength, guidance, sustenance, support—both in the desert and in the desert of our writing. This is the place where, stripped of all the comforts and luxuries, we can begin to really find the inexplicable. We come to know it as love. We fall in love. We are able to have a larger vision, to envision. And we realize the beauty that is there. Sitting in a desert for hours, and especially for days or longer at a time, we become increasingly able to shift from the incredible "emptiness" of a wide view unimpeded by "stuff"—tall trees or buildings—to the magnified, up-close view of a beetle crawling at our feet, the soft patterns in the dirt from a slithering snake, the clear decaying exoskeleton of a tarantula. And these become miracles; the fear we might normally associate with these things is forgotten in the faith, love, and beauty of a burning, on fire desert. spirit burning brightly.

We make a beautiful altar in the desert inspired by the profundity of being able to survive there. We recognize and honor the unexpected gifts we have received through enduring, and then we bow down in gratitude.

Our Spirit's Relationship to Writing

Spirit is nebulous. We can use words to point toward it. But like the map and landscape, the abstract words do a poor job of really capturing the feeling and essence and miraculous unknown of birth and death. Spirit lies in the secret crevice of creativity, intuition, or trickery. Our writing—including the content, the process, the execution of purpose, and the miracle of completion—is absolutely dependent upon faith. Without regard to religion, doctrine, or spiritual perspective—including the conviction, for some, that there is nothing divinely immaterial—we must cultivate, at the very least, a bare modicum of trust as we write. Without faith in *some*thing (even the tiresome belief in "I'll get it done because I have to"), most of us are hard-pressed to accomplish big writing goals. At best, a deep faith in something divine that we adore, practice, and wholeheartedly embrace can elevate us, our writing process, and the outcome in ways that we never could have predicted.

Sometimes we need faith just to return to the page in the middle of that dry desert in our writing: words are elusive, or burned right out of existence. Sometimes we rely on the divine to reveal the next step, even if we can't write out the entire outline of our project. Sometimes the spirit leads us back to the project because it trusts *us* to move ahead, even when we cannot trust ourselves. And when we show up like this—not sure quite what will unfold or how we will ever manage it—with an undefined expectation that exceeds rationality, a spark of something amazing can occur. Our writing becomes imbued with the beauty of something we didn't even know we had inside us, the origins of which we cannot trace to a particular fact, emotion, or physical sensation. Something perfect just lands at our feet (literally, on the writing page). *That* is when we can rest assured that a powerful source has our back.

Essay: Wide Open Sky

It might be the pale, barely-blue blue of an early summer morning with the hint of royal blue beginning to show in the patch directly overhead. Perhaps, instead, it is the grayish sky, smeared with a pretense of weather change but really the same steady ocean mirror if but the clouds were wiped away. The wide, open sky might be that very one that shows itself at dusk, and at dawn: cobalt blue, impossibly colored in the otherwise dim waxing or waning light. I have seen it pure white, like milk spilled upward and impervious to gravity. No matter how it appears, it is the sky: vast, broad, limitless. It looks as if it is *something*, and yet it is just a gaze off into the infinite—appearing to have hue only because of atmosphere—and we call back the little child we were who said, "the sky is blue" with a Crayola of the same name in hand.

We love the sky, and we call to it; the sky hears our prayers and sometimes is the target for them. We find it nearly impossible—even when the ceiling of low dark clouds hovers in steel hunks of rain-awaiting—to imagine that the sky is not "there," not a "thing" with mass, body, and sturdiness. For we always have the opportunity to look up and see, to imagine, to ponder and make fantasy, and to grow our ideas even as our eyes and brains vainly attempt to comprehend the vertical overhead space.

The sky is the backdrop for visual displays and accomplishments of all sorts. Fireworks blasting off in the still-lingering heat of midsummer, coloring "the above" in quickly-shifting kaleidoscopes of reds, golds, whites, sometimes also greens and pinks and oranges. Skyscrapers, so aptly named, appear to touch the sky, especially in places like Seattle, where clouds reach down as much as buildings rise up. Mountain peaks are covered in snow or clouds, or stand prominently waiting to grow tall enough to brush their edges along the curve of the universe. Children and playful adults cloud bust: imagining ever shifting shapes and forms in clouds that dot or clump into rabbits-then-a-bouquet-then-marching-ducks in the heavens. Shooting stars, moons, planets, satellites, and space stations tell stories of places only science fiction can depict, or by way of our own good and healthy vision. Rainbows appear to arch their backs into the celestial sphere; humans remember stories and promises in religious lore.

Even as I type this amidst interruptions in my day, the sky has moved from morning blue to daytime blue, the difference between soft and striking, between serene and exhilarating. The sky is a vast palette for the imagination, for the paintbrush of the mind. It instructs, teaches, inspires, mentors, guides. The blue above me holds and contains and, paradoxically, seems to expand into the inconceivability of eternity. It is both a container and a ceaseless emptiness. I empty myself into the azure above—dreams, fears, worries, excitement—because the vastness that is the un-edged, unconstrained, boundless, and unspeakably huge emptiness above me can encompass all that a person can offer up … and all persons, and all offerings, for all time. The human is too small to grasp the enormity of the eternal, ongoingness of what stretches up there, out there, over there, to where?—but she is large enough to generate endless beseechings and gratitudes that fill the firmament. How deeply cerulean the sky would be if each human on the planet colored even a single coin of sapphire-blue gratitude onto its make-believe surface each day.

Sitting under the heaviness of a sky blackened with drenching rain can feel claustrophobic or liberating; lying down on the ground with face turned straight up offers consolation or anxiety. Because the sky is constant. It is what the human presence inscribes onto it, and ascribes to it, that makes it seem some way or another for him. Why not use that energy, the never-ending potential, that stretch of anythingness, as a turnstile for writing?

*   *   *

The writer sits in a chair on the edge of the lawn or, even better, lies on her back on the grass. She turns her gaze upward and notices a color: a sweeping and marbled sky filled with edges and texture, lines and curves, as the nearby things make a cross section of what is visible above. Filling in empty space, the writer begins to imagine a writing life that is as expansive as the heavens. Anything goes. Anything counts. Everything is valuable toward the goal of writing.

Writing is attitude and perspective, courage and hope, it is usually also dotted with the spicy hot pepper of flair or flailing fear. The act of writing is getting words onto a page. But that is only the very barest and thinnest conception of writing. Writing is a process, an unfolding, a reaching out, an offering, as much as it is an event or behavior. The deception is that writing is "too": too much, too hard, too insignificant, too raw, too easy, too academic or heady or intellectual, too polished, too impersonal, too vulnerable, too constrictive, too flimsy, too important, too much investment, too useless, too limiting, too inconclusive, too bourgeois, too wasteful, too educated, too poetic, too inactive, too solitary and isolating, too little return, too old-fashioned or archaic, too boring, too creative, too literal, too unaffecting, too selfish. It is none of these. Or it does not have to be.

Writing can be alive. It can be: purposeful, vital, endearing, helpful, instructive, invigorating, life-giving, sustaining, crystalline, grounding, complex, sturdy, empathetic, broadening, incredibly basic, modern and current and cutting-edge, balanced, contagious, beautiful, challenging, a birth of all that we dreamed but feared, the very foundation on which our survival rests. Writing breathes and moves in fluid rumbles of thunderous, life changing, clapping applause and affirmation. Writing can be however the writer shapes it in the depths of her being. Like the sky above, writing offers choices and varying views.

Taking one long deep breath in, the writer stretched out on the grass inhales the sweet and enduring fragrance of millions of not-sharp blades of vegetation. She recalls other lifetimes in similar poses: her child-self secretly chewing sourgrass with a friend, telling each other naughty secrets about the false origins of the grass' taste. Her mind leaps to another time on grass, this reverie is tainted with the fresh scent of love: a college sweetheart wrapping arms around her, both too excited and awkward to relax deeply on the earth; in fact, the ground is the setting only, and neither pays much attention to anything that is growing outside of their budding love. And today she finds herself here again, on another patch of green growing stuff, this time the yard she grew out of barren dirt just a few years ago. This time the writing stakes are higher, but she knows she is up to the task. All she needs to do is surrender, trust, and write until she cannot drag one more word from within her to the page—the burden of pages-completed having wearied her beyond expectation.

Every writer can have these moments of quiet, of sweet recall, of substantial hope—from the very grass and sky enfolding her—that she will make her imprint on the page, words carrying meaning and lifeblood, toward the writing goal to which she aspires. Even for the city dweller there is sky to be had, to be glimpsed, to be found beneath. Yea, the sky finds us, calling and asking that we open up as wide as we can; it begs us to stretch out underneath the blanket of blue and rest in what we know is ours to offer. Again, the form and structure, the requirements for the written outcome, do not matter at all in this moment. They are not worth paying attention to when we have the limitless turquoise sky as our guide. The real task is to see the sky. To feel its presence. To acknowledge its ongoingness and the very non-entity-ness of it.

There is never a time in all of one's breathing life that there is no access to the sky. Windows offer views of the sky to shut-ins, the institutionalized infirm; the agoraphobic, even, can find respite in the small patch of sky that sneaks in between the folds of the drawn curtains, becoming visible in the gap between the two sides of the fabric. The very unwavering presence of sky in our lives makes us feel that there is stability, something to hold onto, even though the very thing to which we cling—the idea that there is a material "sky"—is an ethereal one.

When was the last time you doubted the sky? Was it during a storm when you rejected the notion of the very goodness of the heavens, immersed as you were in the dark, wet cold? Perhaps, *was it?*, when you were given the writing assignment against which you now clench your jaw and solidify fists of hands in argument against the idea that writing can accomplish anything much except an afternoon—or days or weeks—of torture and boredom? Maybe the wise among you wondered how you ever, in one or two lifetimes, imagined you could write something as tender as your own good story. There might even be a few of you who are reading this under duress—pressure from somebody else to read this book: a teacher or friend who told or asked you to—or a desperate sense that if you can just find one saving grace in this entire manuscript-of-a-book that perhaps you will find your own nugget to cling to in order to write.

But the sky is vast. The heavens are eternal. The sky, or absence of something up there—that which we have come to call "sky" and labeled as "blue"—is one spirited and everlasting realm of insight and potential, of heartache-assuaged, of answers to queries, of direction in the face of feeling lost. The moment we begin to imagine that there is solidity or only one right answer to our writing problem, we lose the whole notion of the sky's healing and miraculous serum for productivity. We must trust that there is something out there, beyond ourselves, beyond the edge of what we call the sky. We must refrain, in so long as we are able, from naming or identifying too closely with what we perceive as "the answer" or "the solution." I can hear it already: the yelling, "How in the world can I write this assignment, book, memoir, poem, article, letter, thesis, essay by believing in the vastness of a sky that you say isn't there anyway?" Because it takes faith ...

I have a friend. He really wants to believe in something. But he just cannot bring himself to do so. Self-proclaimed an atheist, he has rejected everything his family (in his childhood), his friends (in his youth), and his mentors (in his adulthood) have offered to him as shining gifts of inspiration. This man is absolutely sure that he wants to have faith; he can even see how out of control he can get when he relies on nothing but himself. Yet, he is indelibly marked with an insistent and not-very-endearing stubborn streak that pushes him right back into his head every time he says he wants to hear his heartbeat.

Faith lives in the heart, or at least very deep down in the gut. We do not believe in a sky, or a higher power, or our own ability to craft words onto a page without some measure of faith. This requires us to open up to a possibility with no ground, no visible edge, no material tangibility whatsoever. We can only awaken to faith if we have nothing to rely on but some sense that perhaps—if we are very, very fortunate and providence rains down on us—we will be able to compose the written thing that haunts, tortures, beckons, seduces, threatens, or otherwise stands in our way between now and finished.

So this man I know just keeps on talking to other atheists and doing research of various sorts, and reading all kinds of books. He has a roadmap to his heart, but instead he is using the well-worn pathway back to his intellect to try to "solve" his faith problem. He told me that he wants to believe that he is not alone, that there is something that can help him feel safe and cared for and protected—something that is not human, animal, mineral, vegetable. He is begging and crying for faith and yet he cannot read the signposts that are urging him to let go, to use his guts to get to the destination ... and that it is not an ending place anyway, but rather a sure and solid journey that involves practice and hope even in the face of laziness, ennui, and tremendous fearfulness. This guy is not going to have faith, he says, unless he can absolutely find proof that there is "something" into which he can place his trust. He wants to attach to something.

But faith requires letting go.

�III ⚹ ⚹

So does the sky. It asks us to see something that is not really "there." The sky becomes a beggar asking for the food that will sustain it, that will offer sustenance to our hearts. The icy cold talons of fear are no match for the unfathomable far reaches of space that are beyond the limits of our visual perception. The sky asks us to abandon all that we know with our heads, to simply sit underneath it on a sunny or cryingly-sodden day and trust that it is there: carrying us and letting us find our own way. Held and released. Simultaneously. We experience this earth as large, as impossible to tame by way of knowledge or experience or by traveling to every corner and crack of its surface. The sky is so far beyond that already-incomprehensible scale, that there is no comparison whatsoever. How could we possibly know the earth, much less the sky, when our puny lifetime restricts our ability to thoroughly explore? This is, again, a deal of faith.

All that the sky asks is that we sit or lie beneath it.

I can absolutely tell you that even if you have not eaten one morsel for three full days and have lamely tried to sustain your greedy appetites with a gallon of water for each twenty-four-hour increment, the sky will be there for you. If you sat stark solid alone—no human, no electronics, no computer or bed or tent, barely a bird in the sky, not one single flowering plant—the sky will be there for you. If you abided in a desert of mostly-rock, some skeletons, and enough creepy crawly things to feed your imagination of fear for lifetimes—even if you did that type of solo activity in the wilderness without phones, or vehicle, or friends, or books—the sky will be there for you. It will give you words to scrawl in a shaking, weak hand across a page as dry as the barren thirsty dirt at your feet.

I know this is possible, because this happened to me.

I was out alone on my first wilderness fast with no—absolutely *no*—idea how I had truly ended up out there. (From the comfort of my cushy, warm, safe, easy bed at home—one verdant, misty spring morning months before—in my cute cottage on a little island in the Pacific Northwest, I awoke with the words about a wilderness fast: "I cannot not do it.") I was not yet calling myself "a writer"; I was still in a hopeless and helpless phase of my adulthood: inert, and terrified of all sorts of things. Despite everything I have ever said before and since that fast about "never getting bored," I had already—very literally and amply—cried out of sheer boredom spiced up with a little loneliness. (I am an introvert. I love being alone. But this was totally *different!*) I was bored to tears—many rainfalls and torrents of boredom. And fear. With a little rage thrown in. On this desert fast.

Late on Day Three of this four-day-four-night fasting solo in the middle of Death Valley, a pen jittering in my hungry hand, I was fed faith. I was fed faith in the form of words that I struggled to make coherent on an arid page that ardently sucked at the ink in my writing pen. I was on hour number eighty-four (out of ninety-six) of my solo time and words began to form on the page. The sky—that organ of air stretching, and abiding, and holding me in my solo spot for those four days—offered me some words as I numbly and sadly gazed up into its emerald blue eyes. I was hungry for food for my body. But I was infinitely hungrier for some relief from myself, my thoughts. And that was when I was given faith. It dropped into my lap, and—more precisely—into my journal. And the words that came to me dissolved immaturity, inertia, terror; the words that came to me gave me direction, purpose, hope.

Faith requires silence. It asks for solitude. It does not want anything more from us than openness, a vast willingness to show up to the page, to the task at hand. Like the innocent child we all once were, the calling is to explore the wide territory of firmament and etch that onto the page of our lives.

Wide Open Sky Practice

I urge you, aspiring writer, to go outside. Yes—as always—do not delay or prepare. Just arrive in the outdoor environment surrounding your home place. Go out there alone. Totally alone: no pet, or phone, or book. Just get into air that is fresh and moving. Get very comfortable. Unlace shoes and peel away socks. Plant feet firmly in grass or mud, on top of smooth pebbles, or raise them up to lean against a tree as you lounge on your back. Place your hands on the same surface as your feet for a few moments. When the bending in your body becomes a little bit uncomfortable—or just one second before that moment—stretch yourself out again to a sitting or reclined, flat position out in the natural world. Or the natural garden you have made of the yard. Even venture onto a beach near your home, bundled up against bitter cold wind if you are reading this book in the icy wintertime. Immerse your hands in the little stream that edges the property you have been ever-fortunate to reside upon or visit.

Close your eyes and go stone cold silent. Relaxing into whatever position you have chosen, make your body as absolutely noiseless as you can. Make your mind slow down, like wheels on a bike, getting slower, slower, slower. Get to the place in your head where everything has absolutely stopped. Motionless. Clear, clean, empty. Yes, this is like a meditation: if your brain delivers to you a thought, watch it come and go. Do not add to it another thought. ("This is stupid." —delivered thought. "I'll go inside then and throw away this book." —added thought.) When it seems like you might be drifting into sleepiness, open your eyes easily, effortlessly, and look up at the sky.

Note how big and wide it is. Find the edges of the sky, or at least find the edges of your *view* of the sky. Notice the color: see if you can just look at the color without giving it a name. See if perhaps the sky has other colors instead of "blue"—is there any green, or pink, or white, or tan above you? Watch the sky both intently and lazily. Pay attention to how differently "lazy watching" feels from "watching with intention." Imagine that you have a question to ask, the answer to which will help you move forward with your writing (project). Give words to the question, making it as short and simple as possible. The question about your writing does not have to seek every answer that will "solve" or "complete" your writing problem.

The simple question is the one that asks about the very next step you need to take in the project.

Some examples of questions include: What should I start writing today? Which area of the project needs my attention first? How can I find the motivation to go to the computer today? Where can I get the stamina to stay at the desk long enough to write a paragraph?

You can do this.

Wide Open Sky:

1. Go outside totally alone.
2. Place your naked feet and hands on an earthy surface.
3. Make yourself very comfortable by sitting or reclining.
4. Close your eyes.
5. Quiet your mind until it is empty of thoughts.
6. Now with your eyes open, find the edges of the sky.
7. Notice the sky's colors, but avoid naming those colors.
8. Move between lazy noticing and intentional watching of the sky.
9. Craft in your mind a simple question about your writing.
10. Carry that question back to your writing project.

The Gentler Practice:

1. Go outside by yourself.
2. Look up at the sky.
3. Notice how vast the sky is and how it really has no beginning or end.
4. Think about the vastness of your writing project.
5. Identify one thing you absolutely know about the beginning or end of your writing project. Choose one of these:
    a. Number of pages it should have (if an assignment).
    b. The easier part for you to write (beginning, middle, or end).
    c. How you will know you are done.
    d. When you started working on it (the date).
    e. How much you have left to write.

The Deeper Practice:

1. Follow #s 1-8 in the Wide Open Sky practice.
2. Think about the very hardest aspect of your writing project. Is it any of the following?:
    a. Research you need to do before writing.
    b. Stamina to make it to the end of the project.
    c. Starting.
    d. Finishing.
    e. Grammar, mechanics, structure.
    f. Sources, references.
    g. Making the time to write.
    h. Whatever else you come up with.
3. Remind yourself that your writing project is not larger or vaster than the sky.
4. Think of three questions that come from #2.
5. Use those questions as a way of guiding your next writing session, seeking to answer them as you move through the process of information-gathering and writing.

Essay: Passion Write

Fingers snugly clutch the wet-tipped pen as it glides across the page. It is like being on cross-country skis; an already-carved trail stretches out ahead and the snow is perfect: squeaky-soft and slick. Tall fir trees line the route, boughs still decorated with thousands of white gifts—the flakes from last night's snowfall. Loosely bundled up against the frigidity, free enough to move with ease and grace. It is crispy cold that climbs into the nostrils, hangs off eyelashes, and prickles cheeks. The extensions of appendage underfoot become one with the skier, and there is spiraling beauty in the seamless way snow connects with ski, and ski connects with skier, and skier connects with the surrounding landscape. The separations disappear, as do any thoughts. It is a pure moment untainted with past or future; totally interconnected; no distinction between self and nature, between foot and ski, between stillness and motion. It is abiding in the pure bliss of passion.

*   *   *

Sometimes when we write, we feel stuck. It happens before we sit down, as we begin to craft words into a document, as we set out to engrave our meanings onto the page. There are infinite reasons for this, not the least of which is our lack of enthusiasm for what we are writing, what we are "supposed" to write, what we are mandated to write (which can often stand in between what we love and the words we put on the page). Like a taloned beast, the boredom and lack of interest in what we are trying to convey in words will tear us and our writing—and the very page itself—into tiny shreds. We will be left sitting there wounded, with nothing to show for our efforts but unusable scraps of a thing. Disinterest in what we are writing is not only the bane of every writer, but the final downfall. This is especially true for students writing to an assignment, for writers who feel they—and their good writing—must fit into some mold, for those a bit less skilled in tapping into the wellspring of delight that lives within us all and bringing it to the surface in the symbols we call "words." I have literally wept at the clumsy, trudging, superficiality of something I spent too long composing. And it was not a composition—lyrical and melodic. That was the very trouble with it: it did not make my heart sing.

I have worked with people of all ages, in myriad life circumstances, and with varying relationships to their writing. Some had to write business documents, others school papers, still more were working on personal histories filled with deep emotion, and some writers were piecing together complex and lengthy projects. The moment a writer gets the idea that something *must* fit a specific, particular written format, she has taken a step away from her deep interests. This has been true with each of these paralyzed aspiring writers. He has stepped into a misconception, a preconceived notion of "good and bad," stale forms and stagnant ideas, forgetting and denying the truth of the very project.

When I was writing my candidacy documents for my doctoral degree—that is, attempting to create documents that would be passable; approvable by my committee; and which would allow me the entrée into my own professional status, recognition, research, my very *life*—I felt stuck. Totally and completely immobilized. This is not my M.O. in writing; I had been crafting poetry, essays, stories, research papers, scholarly analyses, memoir, summaries, journals … for decades. But it happened then because I was approaching the writing out of fear as well as some unspoken, intangible idea of what that writing should look like. I was not in touch with my passion; I was writing in mechanized movements and some preconceived notions about what would be considered "suitable." I had set an unreasonable standard for myself, and one that I had totally imagined with no outside referent. Every time I sat down to write I felt nauseated, cramped, agitated, and antsy. One day I had an idea: I would add in a paragraph at the beginning of each section of the document and this would be my place for creative writing. I did not, for one single moment, imagine that these paragraphs would become part of the final written work. I simply knew in my gut that the research I had done (about which I was struggling to write) had been a heart work, infused with enthusiasm and joy. I figured if I just spent a few minutes reminding myself what the experience of being with the craftswomen had been like, I could then write the "dry" stuff that I assumed was required of me. Oh, and those sections I crafted of my memories sitting in a remote village of African artisans (my research "subjects") flowed and danced and sang their way across the pages. Incidentally, those reverie passages ended up staying in the final, approved version of the document; a few years later it was picked up and published by a small, academic press.

Remembering what it is that tingles your skin, puts butterflies of delight in your guts, that enthuses, propels, motivates, animates, that smiles the soul and opens your heart is the key. It will be the very thing that makes whatever written task looms large overhead into a pet—a project that can be swaddled, caressed, embraced. It really is magic. I urge you, Writer, to try it.

Passion Write Practice

Open the computer document that is your required writing task for the day. Let it stand there empty, blindingly white, stark, and creepy. Be sure it has a title and a place to "live" in the docs file. Hit the "save" function so that it is really in the file for the project that needs attention. Close the document but keep the file list open (the "finder" window on most computers). Open the journal that is the friendly and safe place to write; this is the private book that nobody sees. It lives in a special, cloistered, closeted location near your bed and nobody except you has access to it. For those who live with somebody, who feel they need to share every little bit of themselves with their intimate other, please take great caution and allow the privilege of self and soul to have a sacred privacy. I do not advocate the keeping of secrets; I am merely suggesting that we each allow ourselves the honor and dignity of retreat, the sanctity of solitude and quiet. For these are holy and necessary for the spirit to heal, to grow, to thrive.

When the journal is open and the pen of choice (the one that makes your unique signature look especially nice) is in hand, close your eyes. Imagine something that you love, that deeply moves you, or that offers you great excitement. Hold that image, person, desire, dream, fantasy, location in your mind's eye and look closely at it. Find every detail and color, the textures that make that particular thing so pleasing and enticing to you. Play with it a little bit and watch how it (or s/he) can do things not possible in "real" life. Imagine your beloved pet speaking in words to you. Create a natural area that you've never seen that has all your favorite land features in it: an ocean beach with bright yellow water and purple weeping willows growing right up out of the sand. Allow your fingertips to feel the textures, your toes to wiggle in the sand under your feet, or your tongue to lick the saltwater.

Slowly open your eyes just enough to see the journal page in front of you. Spend five to ten minutes describing all of this in your personal book. Embellish it with non-fact: things that might not be actually true, but which feel good. Write in whatever style or format comes easily to you. Compose the words into a circle or spiral shape instead of lines across the horizontal page. Add stick figures or drawings. Pick up a few nearby pens of different colors and add a wash of orange, green, or highlighter yellow. Most of all, have fun with it! If it makes you giggle, then let the belly laugh come; if it makes you swoon, allow yourself to slump over in melodramatic overwhelm. You can do this because nobody will see you, nobody will read your journal, no one will steal or photograph, or mimic you, or criticize this moment. It is yours. Solely for you.

Now, immediately, put down all the pens, pick yourself up from the desktop where you feigned a faint, gingerly lay aside the book, and open up that document. Put your fingers on the keyboard (index fingers on 'F" and 'J') and just sit for a quiet moment. Feel the passion, joy, humor in the prior moment and, at the same time, recall to mind the topic of the document you need to write. (It is right in front of you, in the name of the document.) As soon as you hear a word in your head type it out; let more words come. Do not pay any attention to the beginning, middle, or end of the paper: essay, chapter, article, research section. Just write. Allow your head and heart to melt into a unified whole by keeping the passion of the prior moment alive and intact as your mind finds the words for the written project.

Passion Write:

1. Open the computer document that you need to work on.
2. Be sure it has a title and is saved in the appropriate folder on your desktop.
3. Pick up your journal and pen.
4. Close your eyes and imagine something you love, picturing it in your mind.
5. In your imagination, see this being or thing in full detail.
6. Softly open your eyes and for five to ten minutes, write down as much as you can about these details.
7. Play with the facts or details, totally enjoying the act of writing.
8. Now, put down the journal and pen, and turn to the document on your computer.
9. Sit for a quiet moment with your fingers on the keyboard, recalling the joy of what you love.
10. Type any words that come to you as you begin working on your writing project.

The Gentler Practice:

1. Sit down with a piece of paper and pen.
2. At the top of the page, write down three people or things you love.

3. Set a timer for five minutes.
4. Choose *one* of your three beloveds as your writing focus.
5. Make a list or write simple sentences about why and how you love that one person or thing.
6. Now begin work on your writing project.

The Deeper Practice:

1. Follow #s 1-8 in the Passion Write practice.
2. Using some of the same words and phrases from your passion writing, begin work on your writing project.
3. Foster a feeling of love for some aspect of the writing. Turn your attention to that particular part of your paper, manuscript, essay; write out of pure joy for that piece of the content.

Essay: Nature Altars

Beauty can make us whole. It can fill something within us that nothing else can. Sometimes beauty is a feeling, sometimes an artifact. Other times it walks right up to us, all shiny and aglow, and we are blind to it because we are distracted by the ordinariness of daily burdens. Or we are running so fast through the precious moments of our day that we miss it: a blur as we speed ahead. And some of this speeding and hyper-vigilance is simply headache producing. Sometimes, I daresay "often," all this to-and-fro-ness just mucks up our potential to rest in beauty, to see the awe and wonder of the small things in our day.

Take, for example, the hummingbird who danced and whirred just inches—yes, *inches*—from my face while I ate my last bite of sautéed vegetables at the patio table a few nights ago.

I see these hummingbirds through my window every day. I watch one particular guy land on the branch of a sparely-leaved tree—the twiggy tree that is choking from the ivy climbing up its trunk. And for some reason the hummingbird has chosen this tree, among many other suitable landing spots, to sit and wait. I see him multiple times a day, numerous days a week. He comes to this limb, just outside my office window, and he pauses—sometimes for a few moments, once for over an hour. I have enjoyed his iridescent teal back and red throat patch. I have photographed him. I have ignored him when the client on my computer screen is in turmoil and needs my steady gaze to steady her hand. I have noticed how he arrives at just the crucial moment in another client's story, reminding us of joy—because of his presence, and because of the joy in the story my client is sharing with me. I have seen this hummingbird, or his kin, come to the backyard too—poking himself into the agapanthus, one six-petaled flower at a time.

But the other night over dinner, with all those other guests at the table, it was within inches of *my* own face that he hovered. Wings all blurry with the energy of staying aloft and in one spot. One radiant flash of red followed by a glowing ocean green of his little thrumming chest. And *this* was my moment of the day, my moment to see the extraordinary in the ordinary: hosts of hummingbirds everyday, but now this one special hovering-near-me miracle.

Things that are pleasing to our senses offer us a break, a much needed respite, from the flurry and din of what we refer to as "life"—the derogatory, secular label we tend to give to responsibility, displeasure, discomfort. But we can choose beauty, and we can choose to call "sacred" any particular event, or moment, or phrase. When we are caught unaware by beauty (serendipitous nature spectacles, for example), we feel especially blessed. But we can be creators of intentional beauty, too; then we become the givers of blessings to ourselves and to others.

Our writing can be beautiful. But sometimes it is a chore, work, or has a structure less amenable to beauty (or so we think). Sometimes it is *not* the source of beauty in our lives. Or sometimes we are just too judgmental about our own writing to see the wonder, shape, color, texture, size, scope, and delicate loveliness of the words we have chosen to string together. Going out in pursuit of beauty, to make beauty— particularly when we aren't feeling pleased by the aesthetic of our written project—can be precisely what we need to bring a sense of beauty back into our lives and back into our writing. Great beauty fills us with feelings of awe, gratitude, or peacefulness. Well-being, completeness, relief are just a few more of the potential by-products of our experience of beauty. When we make something that pleases us, a little bit of its beauty rubs off on us; we *become* more beautiful ourselves. And beautiful *us* rubs off on that which we touch—including onto what we write on the page. Beauty becomes beauty.

Several years ago I worked with a group of graduate students at a large urban park; I challenged them to create something beautiful using only what they found in the area, and without harming the flora or fauna. They cleared a thick dirt area of the oak leaves that had fallen there and then shaped the dusty soil into labyrinthine spirals that they then embellished with pine cones; dried, fallen flowers; pebbles; litter that was on the ground when we arrived; and the oak leaves they had put aside. The students took full advantage of every object they found in the spot where they built, essentially, a nature altar. Masters level students preoccupied with the myriad research writing, scholarly papers, and—ultimately—their extensive thesis writing projects, took an afternoon to create something beautiful together in nature. For several weeks after that event, I received emails from the students telling me how important it had been to them to be part of sourcing beauty.

I have been building nature altars for many years. By "altar" I simply mean a special or sacred-to-me grouping of items, usually exclusively from the natural world; almost always, my altars are temporary—built with the intention of impermanence, and the expectation that weather or small critters will disturb and eventually destroy my creation. A few years ago I built an impromptu nature altar under an oak tree at the local off-leash dog park. Several dogs came by to sniff and step in the little "acorn nest" I had gathered; I was humored by this. The following day I returned to that particular location to find that remnants of my project remained, albeit in a bit of disarray. I also built two altars at a nature preserve nearby; a return visit a week later revealed one altar that had been completely rummaged through and was barely recognizable, and one that was in perfectly intact condition. Both were on land far from the river's impact. I accept and honor these transformations. If I need an altar to remain in a pristine state for any amount of time, I alter the conditions by which I create it; this also often entails tending to the altar (removing leaves that blow onto it, refreshing wildflower bouquets, adding lush greens where the original grasses have dried out). Always, I leave my project feeling lighter, freer, more smoothed out.

Nature Altars Practice

The primary "purpose" of building a nature altar is to be as spontaneous as possible so that the creative process can unfold. Allow yourself an open-ended amount of time. Wear comfortable casual clothing and weather-appropriate gear and footwear (or bare feet!). Decide ahead of time where you will create your nature altar. Will you drive to a nearby beach or forest? Walk to the neighborhood park? Or simply wander into your own backyard? There are no requirements on outcome or location. Try to keep your expectations for the final product to a minimum. The ritual is most meaningful when you can let go ...

When you have arrived in the outdoor space, take a few minutes to breathe deeply. Feel what the air temperature does to your skin; notice if the air is still or moving. Glance around at the space noting the foliage and plants, ground cover, rooted things, and fallen things. Gaze up into the sky and peer around corners. Change your usual perspective by sitting or lying down, or kneeling with your eyes close to the ground. What do you see and smell? How does that tiny pebble or new shoot in the grass or pattern in the mud feel as you gently touch it with the tip of your index finger, or with the inside of your wrist? Determine the four cardinal directions in your location. If you are not accustomed to doing so by noting the sun's location in the sky at a particular time of day, use a compass. (The unwritten assumption is that you will not have any electronic devices with you as you make your altar. Honor the sanctity of nature, and the effort and time you are expending, by doing this activity alone and uninterrupted.)

Next, pay attention to the smaller spaces in the area; scope out where you might be able to erect your altar. You can use a boulder with a flat horizontal plane, or an area of mud that is not grass-covered. Consider using that base of the tree over there, or the nearly-hidden patch of ground under that rock ledge or under the bush's branches. Conversely, perhaps you want to choose the wide, open meadow in the center of the natural space. If you are in a sandy, snowy, or muddy place, figure out how you might shape those substances to hold an altar or to build the architectural foundation for it.

Now begin to look for natural items lying on the ground. Seeds and pods, rocks, grasses, weeds, twigs, feathers, wildflowers. Seek those items that have fallen or which typically rest on the ground. Please do not "dismantle" the natural world around you; avoid, for example, uprooting plants or damaging—by cutting, yanking, ripping off their living beings—leaves, branches or flowers. If you are strongly called to use a sprig of sage or a few flowers off a nearby plant, follow the courtesy of asking that living being for permission; then collect the few items as a forager: not taking all of what you see, and spacing out your collections to minimize visual impact and maintain biological integrity. Absolutely do not remove or "relocate" any creatures—snails, sea life, turtles, or frogs—or disturb any homes in use (i.e., nests, dens, gopher holes). Make a small pile of the items you would like to use for your altar.

Consider the shape you would like to use. (I seem to be utterly drawn to circles; so far every altar I have erected—with the exception of rock cairns—has been circular.) You can stack the items, spread them evenly over a surface, place some inside or outside a particular "boundary" on the altar. For example, if you have created a circle out of small stones as the foundational structure of the altar, you might line the inside of that pebble circle with a layer of leaves. Maybe the most special item you have found (like the silky clean blue jay feather) will earn its place in the center of the altar. Whenever I do this activity, I tend to use the most plentiful items around the edges, placing the fewer or singular items nearer the center. The most germane instruction for this part of the ritual is to *follow what is pleasing to your heart.* Follow what looks good to you. Think about the significance of the items you have placed there. You might decide to put objects into similar-colored groupings, alternate colors, or arrange them in gradations of color (autumn leaves sequenced from reds to oranges to yellow). Use textures you like. Make it full of objects if that seems good to you, or spare if that feels better. Do what makes your heart soar.

Spend as much or as little time as you like creating your nature altar. Avoid judgments: *If only I had ..., It's too ..., What will _____ think ...* The only criterion for completion is that you engaged the process. Even if you do not prefer the outcome, congratulate yourself for this first (or second, or fifth) attempt. When you go out to do this practice again (remembering that "practices," by definition in this book, are *repeated*), consider making it simpler if you left the prior practice with a negative feeling about the outcome. I have seen a single simple rock, aesthetically placed, that "counts" as a nature altar. Be sure to draw or photograph the altar after each construction.

I like to share my altar with a special person; I choose somebody who is open to the process and idea—who won't make negative judgments about it. I also like to visit my altar over time. It is especially important to me to see how the weather, elements, wild creatures, and time make their mark on my creation. Sometimes I dismantle my altar within a day or two. Sometimes I create it near the tide line so that the ocean can slowly carry away the items. Whether or not you share your altar, or visit it, is up to you.

Nature Altars:

1. Arrive at the outdoor space you have chosen for your nature altar project.
2. Spend a few minutes seeing and feeling what is around you in that space.
3. Seek out a good place to build your nature altar.
4. Search for items that you can use to create your altar.
5. Pile them up near the site you have chosen.
6. Consider the shape and size of your altar.
7. Then begin to craft it, paying attention only to what pleases you.
8. Avoid judgments about the outcome.
9. Draw or photograph the altar.

The Gentler Practice:

1. Go outside your home to an area with plants, trees, or grass.
2. Search for three or four interesting or pretty fallen natural items. Perhaps you see three oak leaves and an acorn.
3. Gather these gifts from nature and arrange them in a simple pattern on the ground or at the base of a tree.
4. Draw or photograph your beauty.

The Deeper Practice:

1. Follow #s 1-8 in the Nature Altars practice.
2. Consider how the springtime contributes to this altar.
   a. Does it face east?
   b. What season is it right now?
   c. How does the new life of spring give gifts that are on your altar now?
3. Sit down in front of your altar once you have completed it.
   a. What is it telling you about your own expression of beauty?
   b. What can you learn by sitting quietly with a soft gaze?
4. Do a short meditation at your altar.
5. Draw or photograph the altar.

Chapter Seven

THE BEAUTY OF WHOLENESS

This book has sought to demonstrate how vital balance is in our pursuit of writing, as well as in our pursuit of life. And that balance is not a pros and cons sheet with neatly listed items in columns. Nor is it a sum game involving quantities—adding up, deleting—in order to achieve some sort of numerical equivalence or sameness. Sometimes balance is about just gritting our way through until we are restored to a sense of completeness about an issue, problem, or grief in our life; sometimes it means rediscovering who we are after a major life change. Restoring balance can look like extended periods of play, recovering from trauma, seeking out spiritual retreats, or navigating grueling graduate study. And how we refocus, restore, and re-story ourselves to come back into vibrant equanimity is the process of claiming wholeness. In other words, what we seek is a sort of *quality* of balance: things naturally change, but we remain alright because our experience of life deepens through those transitions.

Through the perspectives of body, emotion, mind, and spirit, we have explored together the sense of wholeness that we can feel when we engage a few simple practices. Allowing these four aspects of ourselves to be part of our writing does enrich the form, process, content, and outcome of our projects. It also affords us a sense that we are living a bit more in harmony with our biggest, truest selves. Writing really does become more naturally ours as we begin to deepen and reconnect with the natural world, and thus, our human nature.

You have now had the opportunity to explore six writing and six nature-based activities. But do not stop with a single attempt. Remember that a practice is something we do frequently and repeatedly. We watch it shift over time. Some days we wake up in a fog of worry or discontent. Other times we take our first conscious and deep inhalation of the morning and we thank the world for giving us another beautiful, ordinary day to experience the tenderness of this exquisite world.

*   *   *

When writing does not feel bad, it feels really delicious.

A quick dip into the cool river on a scalding hot day. The moist respite of a wooded grove. The views from a mountaintop at the end of a long upward hike. An opening out of the landscape and a feeling that one can breathe deeply after the claustrophobic tightness of a rushing interstate in the city. One sun-warmed blackberry juicing itself on the tongue, plucked from between the thorny spines late in the afternoon ... a slight purplish stain on thumb and forefinger the last vestige of the forager's delight. The full harvest moon delightfully round, smiling—beaming—as it rises into view. The tingle of warmth stepping nearer the fire on a frigid midwinter night. Or wildflowers—shockingly yellow, by the hundreds— that suddenly appear one day in the once-just-grassy field.

Writing something can feel like a step toward a more whole self. It can feel like a lifetime accomplishment. It can be relief—sweeping, vast, broad—after a cold, dark time afraid and alone. Lonely, even. The writing process, as well as the written thing, can seem like a companion on the journey, the one who has the courage to convey what the writer cannot possibly ever speak aloud. Writing takes on a life of its own; we hear accomplished authors say this over and over again. It bears repeating. It is true. Writing begets writing. The more it does so, the better it feels to the writer. Sometimes the person whose hand is the instrument of the words coming forth onto the page is oblivious to the power of the words, or even unaware what she is writing until it has been fully brought forth.

Like froth on the roiling ocean, writing is ever-changing, rising up, receding, but always a body there for us. Even when we are not putting our hands, eyes, arms, fingers in service to the words that tug at our cuffs, writing is present. With us always. Perhaps that is why it feels so completing to manifest them on the page. A part of us comes alive, breathing as we breathe, and we feel that a new thing has emerged. Yet writing from our deepest selves is as old as the hills, ancient, traditional, primal. Just as we gently etch our caress along the cheek of a loved one, so too our writing writes itself from our inner life to our outer one and in so doing brings us together, fully, united. In love.

I am in love with writing. This does not mean that it is easy for me. Or all-the-time-enjoyable, pleasant, sensible. It does not mean that I write my guts out onto the page and then say, *Ah, it is finished. Writing begets writing.* And it also begs for attention. Like a new lover crazy and craving attention, writing hugs and enfolds and kisses us with its sometimes-too-much ferocious love. I give it time and attention—all that is its due, I imagine. But the moment I leave the page, I hear its siren call begging me back. Like a romance that I don't want to ever end—like the lips on lips that warmly entice—writing seduces me. It is so full of passion—I am so full of passionate insanity—that we each resist the parting even knowing we will be reunited again the next day. Or in a few hours. Writing embraces me fully, tightly, endearingly. He is present in my heart, even when I am attending to others. A word or phrase. An idea of how the chapter will unfold. An organizational detail that bridges the gap between what I didn't know a moment ago and what I won't know in an hour. A step toward the next bit.

And passionate writing does not come all at once, although its force and power and hold on me feel all-consuming in any instant. It is bursts of inspiration or a few sentences or an idea that comes paragraph by paragraph. It is a landscape of living, day to day, that is filled with the perfection of beauty: deeply rooted trees, birds' nests with a new egg each day, that first warm spring day, an autumn's initial rain pour. Perfection is not flawlessness; it is allowing for the wholeness—of dark and light, unattractive and gorgeous figures, in-progress and polished work—to flourish at each stage. It is the letting in of something just as it is, the words on the page arriving however they do, and trusting that it is what it needs to be at this moment, with more to come. Passion and perfection merge in writing when process is the mantra. Practice becomes the *modus operandi*, and expectations fall away. It is pure, unadulterated being: writing that which comes, and knowing that later is later when editing is necessary. It is being right now with the work, with the words, with the fingers scrambling across the keyboard searching for just the next thing to put, letter by letter, onto the waiting white space.

Perfection and passion are not, in writing, what we know them to be in life. Passion is the driving force; perfection is the acceptance that whatever is coming out is what needs to emerge. This does not mean we don't edit later. It just means that to generate words on the page, we must be fully in tune with now. Right now.

The landscape is also bliss for me.

Through deserts and meadows; seven continents of flora and fauna; ponds, springs, snowfields, rivers, glaciers, estuaries; the tundra of mountain peaks; windstorms or calm; deep within caves or deep below the surface of the sea; in, atop, below, or beside deciduous and coniferous trees; in four seasons over five decades I have sought out natural places. I abide in them. My hand reaches for the fur, nape, or soft breath of nonhuman creatures. I measure days, weeks, and months by adding a small object from nature to a round palette each day. My body is well, healthy, whole, strong, invigorated, relaxed in nature's sweet places. My emotions become smoothed, less intense, when I allow myself to rest in nature's havens. My mind becomes fresh and clear, or is stimulated by the wealth of knowledge contained in a single stamen, the coyote's eye, the antennae of a slug. My spirit remembers awe and is inspired by frequent, prolonged abidance in nature's cathedrals.

Work is impossible for me if it does not include some element of ecology. Days off are muted and laid to waste if I cannot get outside to roam or sit. Every creative project I have ever aspired to contains either images of or resources from the natural world. My hospice volunteer service revolves around one of the most natural (and inescapable) Earth journeys of all: the dying process. And each time I have needed any kind of healing myself, it is to nature that I turn.

Not only that, nature has shown me: who I am, and what compassion is, and how to be free, and why it all really matters.

The infinite riches in the outdoor nature storehouse mirror the expression of humanity.

Many years ago when I was challenged to deepen my faith in the unseen divine, I told my mentor that I could not live without direct contact with nature's beasts and beauty. In that moment of speaking those words I had always known but never uttered, I was filled with overwhelming reverence and gratitude: creation is holy! I immediately retrieved my journal and pens from the basket beside my favorite chair and I began to write it all down—how nature gave me life, how nature is life, how nature saved my life, how nature takes life ...

Writing and nature merge, converge, overlap, subsume one another in turns. They are inseparable. Undeniably and inextricably interconnected. Words and landscapes interact, engage, and feed each other.

I walk out into the landscape with a journal tucked under my arm and a pen in my hand ...

*   *   *

I deeply thank you for journeying through the terrain of writing and nature with me. I trust that you are headed out your own door to explore what is wild and growing around you. May you return from this sojourn in the natural world with an energized body, a full and open heart, a clear mind, and faith that you will be given exactly what you need. With your paper stretched out before you, may your pen walk into the landscape of rich words to convey what is wild and growing *within* you ...

About the Author

Jennifer J. Wilhoit, PhD is an author and spiritual ecologist. She works as an editor, writing and life mentor, consultant, researcher, educator, & peacemaker; Jennifer is also a longtime hospice & bereavement volunteer. Her books, articles, & blogs focus on the human/nature relationship— what she calls "the inner/outer landscape." Jennifer founded *TEALarbor stories* through which she compassionately supports people's deep story processes via writing, nature guiding, creativity, life transition & grief support, & mediation. In addition to her individual practice with clients, Jennifer also offers presentations, workshops, trainings, courses, & retreats. She is a partner with the Charter for Compassion & faculty of their Compassion Education Institute. When she is not writing or working, Jennifer hikes, makes beauty in & photographs natural landscapes; reads; travels (internationally, as often as possible); & dabbles in creative arts. Jennifer thrives in the beautiful Pacific Northwest landscape where she lives.

CPSIA information can be obtained
at www.ICGtesting.com
Printed in the USA
FSOW03n0728070318
45412FS